PLAN B

THE *REAL DEAL GUIDE* TO CREATING YOUR BUSINESS

KATHLEEN RICH-NEW

NEW YORK

PLAN B
THE *REAL DEAL GUIDE* TO CREATING YOUR BUSINESS

ISBN 978-1-61448-378-6 paperback
ISBN 978-1-61448-379-3 eBook
Library of Congress Control Number: 2012948149

Morgan James Publishing
The Entrepreneurial Publisher
5 Penn Plaza, 23rd Floor,
New York City, New York 10001
(212) 655-5470 office • (516) 908-4496 fax
www.MorganJamesPublishing.com

In an effort to support local communities, raise awareness and funds, Morgan James Publishing donates a percentage of all book sales for the life of each book to Habitat for Humanity Peninsula and Greater Williamsburg.

Get involved today, visit
www.MorganJamesBuilds.com.

TABLE OF CONTENTS

INTRODUCTION

THERE ARE BETTER OPTIONS for making a living other than being subjected to the whims of other people—people called bosses. A job, also known as your Plan A, does have a steady paycheck but it usually comes with the requirement to follow certain rules and endure mounting pressure to work harder and faster. In the end, no matter how hard you work, there is no guarantee you will keep your job or your pension. I know, I've been there.

Most people I know are talented, smart, and hard working; they just need a road map to help them take control of their lives. My own years of experience in corporate America and my research into businesses sometimes took me to places I never expected—places I call rabbit holes. I had to stop and ask, "How did I get here?" and "How do I get out of here?" By studying successful businesses and those that failed, I came to understand the common key ingredients most successful businesses have, and I figured out how to expand a simple idea into a full-blown business by using the Real Deal Checklist that I created.

My journey to creating my own new Plan B career— one that became both profitable and that I love—helped me realize how conditioned we all are to accept the status quo. We stay in a job, even if we feel trapped by it, with little or no understanding of how to create our own future. Because I had no idea how to create a Plan B, I went down a lot of those rabbit holes. I eventually learned the hard way what we need to know, ask and do to create a new successful Plan B career. Learning those lessons helped me to develop the content you now hold in your hands.

A Few Rabbit Holes Can Be a Good Thing

This book is the means for you to create your own Plan B—one where you control your own future and your own fun, too. You'll see how successes can come to you, although it won't be fast or easy. The information in this book will prepare you for the rabbit holes you'll encounter, although you'll go down fewer of them because you are learning from my trial and error. And, by the way, there *will be* rabbit holes; they are part of the journey. And exploring a few rabbit holes is actually a good thing, as you'll see.

So keep reading to see what extraordinary opportunities are possible for you.

A World of Wisdom and Tips— All in One Place

I am on a mission—a mission to help people avoid the pitfalls of making wrong (and costly) decisions when they realize they need a new way to create income. Perhaps their Plan A job was eliminated, or they are burned out from the work they do, or they're already retired but find their money is running out. When that happens— or, even better, before it does—it's time to create a Plan

B. A Plan B puts you in control of your life and your future: a place where no one is holding you back. And I will show you how!

The knowledge you need is not mysterious or difficult to understand. Mostly, it's just challenging to locate. But you don't have to do that work because I already have located it *and* put it all together for you in this book.

This book is packed with checklists and self-assessments that will help you realize your best Plan B options, which will save you significant time, money, and frustration. And get you to where you want to be that much sooner.

Among other helpful tips, you'll read the good and bad news about each of the four paths to creating Plan B income—start a business, buy a business, buy a franchise, and get involved in network marketing. You will also be able to examine the advantages and disadvantages of each of the four options.

I share the stories of real people who have successfully created a Plan B, and there are stories of people whose business ideas did not work out as they had hoped. You can learn from their successes and, more importantly, from their mistakes so you won't make the same ones.

By the time you have finished this book, you will understand the time, money, and resources necessary to be successful for any of the Plan B options. You will think about and answer thought-provoking and useful questions, which will increase your ability to make informed and smart decisions.

Remember: You *can* get rich by developing a Plan B and starting something new, because you will know how to make the right choices.

NASA Space Shuttle Program's End Was Actually a Great Beginning— Who Knew?

The inspiration to write this book came crashing in on me in 2009 as the reality of the end of NASA's Space Shuttle Program was closing in on us in the Space Coast area of Florida (Cape Canaveral, Cocoa Beach, Merritt Island, and Titusville). Although former President George W. Bush announced the end of the program in January 2004, few people believed it would actually happen. But, eventually, it became clear that almost nine thousand people would lose their jobs by 2011. Even worse, many of these employees were decades away from retirement. The majority of those nine thousand laid-off people worked for NASA subcontractors and lived or worked only a few miles from my own small community. Any open jobs in the area were quickly filled, and the job market—and the national economy—were grim.

I knew that most of those stranded employees would not find other jobs, no matter how good their résumés were or how well they handled job interviews. I also suspected that many of them, because they could not find a job, would rush into the first opportunity they thought they saw, without knowing how to do the real analysis and planning. It was a recipe for disaster.

All of this was clear to me because I had gone down the same path more than a decade earlier, when I left my corporate job because I was so burned out. Then, I had no idea what lay ahead and consequently spent several years and a small fortune as I figured out my Plan B. I made mistakes—*so* many mistakes—along the way, but I learned from them.

And now you can too.

Make Fewer Mistakes and Enjoy More Successes

Those mistakes helped me uncover or create the questions we all need to ask ourselves as we decide if creating a Plan B is the right choice—the best journey to embark on. Those mistakes also helped me to discover resources or create the tools you will use to determine if your Plan B idea is strong enough to be competitive and successful. The *Real Deal Checklist,* for example, will steer you through developing the products and/or services you can offer your customers. You will also be able to quickly determine which Plan B option or options will be the best match for you as you determine the particular work lifestyle you want.

Most of us have done what we were told to do by our parents or grandparents: Get an education, find a good job, and work hard. This was our Plan A, and it probably worked for many of us for quite some time. But then we suddenly found ourselves without a job—for whatever reason—and with few options. So, many of us decided to become entrepreneurs and run our own businesses...yikes!

Unfortunately, too many people invest their severance pay or cash out their retirement savings, only to fail in their business-ownership venture *because they did not know what it really takes for a new business to succeed.* The

McDonald's brothers had a local successful hamburger stand in San Bernardino, California in the late 1940s. But it took Ray Kroc to turn McDonald's into an international phenomenon.

Who Will Benefit From a Plan B?

The young and the seniors.
The employed and the jobless.

Many young workers, as it turns out, are keenly interested in a Plan B because they can't find jobs. Because older workers feel the pressure to remain in their jobs longer (due to pension plans failing, personal investments drying up, or real estate values dropping), they continue to occupy the very jobs that younger workers need in order to progress in their careers. On top of that, many of the young workers who do find jobs are told they will have to fund their own retirement and they will not have healthcare benefits when they retire. Even those young workers who do find and commit to Plan A jobs realize that staying with one company for decades does not guarantee an eventual pension payout—which may or may not ever come. Thus, these young people are turning to a Plan B as a way to meet their financial and other life goals.

Retirees and older workers are looking for a Plan B as they find they are outliving their money. Companies are cutting pension payouts not only of their future retirees but also of those who are already retired. Healthcare benefits continue to be cut as companies are forced to reduce expenses.

Other professionals who turn to a Plan B do so simply because they're burned out from the work they have been doing, as I was. This is a common pattern with professionals who have done the same type of work for fifteen, twenty, or twenty-five years. Something happens—usually a personal or professional crisis—and they decide they are fed up, so they start looking around for something new.

But no matter what situation you are in or how secure you feel your job may be, you need to explore a potential Plan B. If you are working in a Plan A job, that's great. Stay there for now, but keep in mind that while it may be your current job, it probably won't be your last one... unless you take charge of your career and your life by creating a Plan B.

This book is the *real deal guide to creating your business* because it shows how to take immediate control of your life and your future in a way that doesn't depend on finding the next job.

This *Real Deal Guide* Shares It All— the Good, the Bad, and the Ugly

For each Plan B path you'll examine (and then choose to either explore or ignore), I will share with you the good, the bad, and the ugly—information that would have been hard for you to find on your own. It's easy, of course, to locate the good stuff, but it takes a lot more work and digging to identify each option's bad and ugly aspects—those that are hidden behind the curtain or swept under the rug. With this book, you'll have the information to create your Plan B faster and more easily— and with better chances for sustainable success—than those who don't.

Even more importantly, this *real deal guide* will help you ask the right questions of yourself and others so you don't wake up and realize six months or a few years from now that you have made a very bad mistake. These are questions I did not have when I started my journey and they would have helped me make better decisions. So I urge you to answer these questions before you start spending any time and money on an idea that you'll likely realize at some point that you can't or won't pursue.

This book is about the reality of owning and running a business—the stuff most schools don't teach you.

My three business degrees—a BS in Business Administration, an MBA, and a Master's in Management—did not teach me what I eventually had to learn on my own as I created my Plan B business. It seems that I attended hundreds of seminars, conferences, and trainings that all focused on the "you can do it," rah-rah approach, and only occasionally would someone reveal the hard work it takes, how long it is until you make a profit, and how much money you actually need.

This is why I created *the real deal guide;* it is all about *full disclosure.*

Here's the bottom line: This is a new economy and we must all adapt to the new reality. Many seemingly secure jobs, companies, and retirement funds have been destroyed. People in their twenties and thirties will probably never know job or career security. Instead of working longer and harder at a job, your future success depends on your ability to become an entrepreneur—to effectively create your own Plan B.

Specific Benefits of the *Real Deal Guide*

Let's get specific. Here's what you will discover in *Plan B* and why it will make creating your own Plan B easier, faster, and more successful:

- "I Worked Hard, I Played by the Rules, *and This Is All I Get?*" validates those of you who have already realized you need a Plan B but don't know how to create one. For people who feel secure in their Plan A jobs and don't think they need a Plan B, this chapter can serve as a wake-up call. We'll take a look at the supposedly secure pensions that are being cut or eliminated, the impact of more people living longer (which takes a lot more money), and when our Social Security program is projected to run out of money. We delve into the topic of jobs that are disappearing due to layoffs and companies closing their doors. These are some of the many reasons why it's time to start creating options to ensure your future is financially safe, and why a solid, well-planned Plan B is your best bet for changing your future.

- "Is Your *WHY* Bigger than Your *BUT?*" helps you create your powerful *why* for a Plan B. You must have a powerful why so you will stay on track when your buts (those pesky doubts, delays, problems or obstacles) happen that would otherwise provide an excuse to lose or shift your focus to less fruitful matters.

  The Life Values Model helps you evaluate which life values you are most dissatisfied with and then pick the one or two you are ready to change. After that, it's easier to identify what you do and don't want in your future. You'll use the results of this important work many times as a guide toward your best Plan B option.

- "The Real Deal about You" introduces the concept of the hero's journey as a way to reinforce the idea that deciding on and starting your Plan B is a journey. Everything will not run as you expect it to, and there will be rabbit holes. We take this idea a step further by applying the hero's journey concept to the real-life story of Holly Wilder, who decided it was time to do something new with her life and went on to create a wildly successful cupcake empire. Read this chapter to find out how Holly decided that cupcakes were her Plan B, how she became a two-time winner on the cable TV show *The Cupcake Wars,* and how she got a contract to write a new cookbook for creating meals and snacks in a cupcake pan.

  This chapter includes the results of research on the key traits of serial entrepreneurs and what motivates them; you'll use this information to analyze and decide which traits you may already have. The five requirements for successful change are explained, so you can learn how to make any necessary changes. I also show you how to determine who to listen to, so you get the right type of guidance and at the right time.

- "There Are Many Paths to a Plan B" starts with an introduction to Shannon Wilburn, a stay-at-home mom who built a $20-million consignment franchise that solved the problem of her kids outgrowing their clothes too fast.

Next, you get a packing list for your journey into the future. The list shows how to develop the type of mindset you'll need, how to identify the right opportunity and the right time, and how to gain the new skills best suited to your Plan B. This packing list will also remind you of the importance of your *why* and help you overcome the *buts*.

To help motivate you and clarify your path to success, we examine interesting statistics on how the Wealthy 1% of the United States' population has made their money, followed by an introductory look at each of the four Plan B options.

- "Thinking It Through—Avoiding the Pitfalls of Wrong (and Costly) Decisions" helps you identify where the time and money will come from to create your Plan B. You decide the work lifestyle you want by identifying your preferred work location and your workday's characteristics, for starters. Then you determine the energy and stamina that will be physically and mentally required from you, what the emotional toll may be. And most importantly by identifying your exit strategy.

- "Six Key Ingredients of the Most Successful Companies" identifies and explains the primary ingredients common among successful businesses. The more of these ingredients you have, of course, the better. To help you understand how to use them, this chapter starts applying these key ingredients to a variety of ideas, products, and services, and to each of the four Plan B options, which we continue doing throughout the book.

- "The Real Deal about Starting Your Own Business" introduces the first Plan B option and provides you with the good and bad news and the advantages and disadvantages of a business start-up. We cover the two types of start-ups and then look at real-life success stories for each of them.

  The Real Deal Checklist makes its début here, showing you how to improve and expand your business idea. We use this checklist as a framework for examining my client Kate's idea to increase the product and service options she will offer in her Plan B consulting business. As we'll continue to do in the next three chapters, we see which of the Six Key Ingredients our real-life Plan B creators can use to further evaluate the strength of various business ideas.

- "The Real Deal about Buying a Business" introduces the second Plan B option and gives you its good and bad news as well as its advantages and disadvantages. Here we apply the Six Key Ingredients and the Real Deal Checklist to a business that Paul, a young professional, wants to buy.

  Next, we take an in-depth look at how to start your search for a business to buy, the financial documents you need to provide and those you will receive and need to review, and the documents you will sign to protect the seller's information. You discover how to conduct your own due diligence by using a company's business listing information and its selling memorandum.

  We discuss why and how business brokers can be helpful and the valid role they often play. Lastly,

I've included a list of the steps involved in buying a business so you know what to expect during the process.

- "The Real Deal about Buying a Franchise" is the third Plan B option. Here, you learn some basic lingo about the franchise industry, and its good and bad news. You learn about its advantages and disadvantages, and the controls and restrictions that franchisors typically impose on their franchisees.

We discuss a variety of types of franchises that are available and the likelihood that there is a franchise for just about any industry you can imagine and want to be part of. The list of questions to ask yourself (which complement the work you will have done in chapters 2 and 5) are extremely useful to determine if buying a franchise is a good fit for you and, if so, which types of franchises will work best.

In the next section, we apply the Six Key Ingredients and the Real Deal Checklist to various types of franchises, and explain the four franchise models.

You learn not only how to find a good franchise by yourself, but also the role a broker plays in selling a franchise, and the advantages and disadvantages of using a professional broker. We examine the differences between a franchise broker and an advisor, as well as the questions to ask when evaluating each of them. I also guide you on how to conduct your own due diligence by using the government-mandated Franchise Disclosure Document (FDD).

This chapter's content will help you decide whether you want to buy a new or an existing franchise. And we take a quick peek at which areas of the franchise industry are growing—always good information to know!

- "The Real Deal about Network Marketing" is the fourth of the four Plan B options. Naturally, this chapter shares the good and bad news about the network marketing industry, as well as its advantages and disadvantages. And, right off the bat, we address the confusion some people have about legitimate network marketing companies versus Ponzi and pyramid schemes (which are illegal).

  Next, you gain knowledge of the typical controls and restrictions network marketing companies impose, the most common types of products and services sold, and what percentage each type occupies within the industry. As always, we demonstrate how to apply the Six Key Ingredients and the Real Deal Checklist to various products so you can determine if a network marketing company's current products are robust and attractive enough for your potential customers.

  Be sure to check out the particularly valuable list of questions to ask yourself as you select the type of network marketing company that best fits your needs and goals.

  After that, we explain the two ways network marketing teams are built and recommend a way to start yours. There is a lot of hype about the many ways you can sell to customers, and this book shares research that indicates which one accounts for 80% of the sales. Of course, we haven't forgotten the importance of making money, so I have included a brief overview of two typical network marketing compensation plans.

As with the other Plan B options, you see exactly how to conduct your own due diligence on a network marketing company and on the people you choose to work with, i.e., your up-line, and why this due diligence can make or break your business—and your sanity.

• "Putting Your Plan B into Action" reminds you of all you have learned in the short space of this book, and I've included more real-life stories of Plan B successes to remind you of what is possible.

In this last chapter, it's time to really get busy! You'll use a simple process with charts to narrow your options to those that you can and will pursue. And you can use the additional resources listed for each Plan B option for more information as you get started.

Lastly, you learn in this chapter how the Plan B concept is helping many people just like you, your family, and your friends.

You Now Have What It Takes

Many people have great ideas but never make a dime from them. This book shows how to do it.

But a word of caution: It is neither quick nor easy. As you read earlier, information in *Plan B* is the result of years of research, interviewing experts, sitting through countless courses, reading volumes of books, spending a bundle of money, and making way too many mistakes on the hero's journey to my own Plan B. As you know, I created my Plan B through trial and error, and it would have been incredibly less painful, expensive, and disastrous if I had had all of the information you now have. You hold in your hands more information about Plan Bs than 80% of the population that is struggling to make their Plan B work. Consequently, you can look forward to sunnier days, more relaxing nights, and a brighter, more satisfying future.

It's time to start your adventure…just turn the page!

CHAPTER 1

I Worked Hard, I Played by the Rules, and This Is All I Get?

LET'S FACE IT, if you are reading this book, you are already in transition. You realize you aren't going to get what you want from what you are doing now. You need a Plan B because your Plan A job isn't working for you. You are starting to lean forward, interested to learn more about Plan B.

Let's define the terms *Plan A* and *Plan B* and the differences between them. Plan A is a job working for a company to earn a paycheck. It is the "working for the man" plan to make money. You pretty much know in advance how much you will earn based on your hourly rate or annual salary.

Plan B, as we use it, refers to the other ways you can make a living that do not involve working for someone else. For example, you may use your experience to start your own company, or you may decide to buy a business. Plan B puts you in charge of your time and the work you do. And you are writing your own paycheck.

During the past three decades the world has changed, and it's not going to change back any time soon. The rules most of us have grown up with have gone out the window. Jobs have been outsourced overseas and they are not coming back. You and many others have arrived at this new reality for any number of reasons. Some people planned all along to work for themselves, but for many others, there is no choice: a job was eliminated, a skill set was no longer needed, or declining health no longer made it possible to continue working at the same job.

Perhaps this all-too-true story will sound familiar because something similar has happened to you or someone you know. Let's use David's situation as an example.

> David, a passionate sales engineer professional, was waiting his turn to find out if he was going to have a job after the latest round of layoffs. He had survived the last two rounds but was worried about this one. Sales were sliding, and management had announced they were going to reduce the number of employees to a fraction of the current staff.
>
> David walked in the door on this particular morning and saw his manager, Jim, and the human resources manager, Stacy.
>
> *"This can't be good,"* he thought. Jim and Stacy stood up. He shook their hands and they all sat down.

Stacy looked straight at David and said gently, "This is going to be a difficult conversation, David. Your position has been eliminated."

David flinched as if he had just been punched in the gut.

"Do you need a minute or would you like us to continue?" asked Jim.

"No, go on," David said. It's not like he wasn't expecting it, but that didn't take away the shock.

Jim and Stacy explained the layoff package and talked about the severance pay, help with his job search, and on and on.

Suddenly, David's rage exploded. He stood, yanked up his right shirt sleeve, and pointed to the company's colorful logo tattooed on the inside of his forearm. "I bleed six colors for this company. I worked hard, I played by the rules, and this is all I get?"

As David learned, loyalty to one company no longer provides job security.

Why Is Plan A Not Working Anymore?

If you're living your Plan A, you may already feel vulnerable because you realize your job could end. That's good—at least you are paying attention. Those who feel safe are either oblivious to today's reality, or in denial. If you know people like that, please give them a copy of this book; they are the ones who need to sit up and take notice.

Plan B is about making plans before you need them. The captain of the *Titanic* probably thought his job was pretty secure…that is, until he hit the iceberg and remembered there were not enough lifeboats for the number of passengers on board. If you don't want to go down with the ship, keep reading and get to work on your Plan B. You never know when your path may encounter icebergs.

With a job—your Plan A—you may be making a living but perhaps your lifestyle is not ideal. You are probably like most people—trading time for money, and perhaps both are running out. You may have come to realize that, although some of your bosses have been brilliant, caring, and competent, leaders in too many organizations are small-minded, self-centered individuals who may say the right things but don't really give a hoot about what happens to you. They are too busy with their own high-pressure, iceberg-filled reality.

All you've really wanted was to enjoy the company of smart, hard-working peers, be mentored by considerate and knowledgeable bosses, and ease into a comfortable retirement lifestyle at an early age. You did what they told you to do: get a good education, get a good job, and work hard. That was your Plan A.

How is that working out for you? I understand any anger. I have been there…

But don't throw this book at the nearest wall! It can be your best friend from this point on. You are about to create your own economic stimulus package by learning how to create your Plan B.

But first, let's see exactly where Plan A went astray. Consider the wisdom of the Greek historian Plutarch:

"To make no mistakes is not in the power of man; but from their errors and mistakes the wise and good learn wisdom for the future."

The Mythical Promise of Plan A (Whatever happened to the gold watch?)

The traditional Plan A has been to work for a company for twenty, thirty, or forty years and get a lifelong pension and health care benefits. Traditionally, Plan A had a contingency for job loss; you simply go on a job search for a replacement job. Some of you may find a replacement job and be able to continue with your Plan A. Or you may find the replacement job's pay is a fraction of what you were making. And, for many, there simply are no replacement jobs. An associate's, bachelor's, or master's degree might get you a job, but there are no guarantees.

In fact, it is estimated the average person today will have changed jobs seven to ten times in their lifetime. An interesting statistic I heard recently is that the average twenty-two-year-old will change jobs twelve times by the time they are thirty-eight years old. The driving force behind this churn is the rapid advance of technology coupled with the culture shift involving the human dynamics of technology dependence.

Those in their twenties and thirties will likely never know job or career security. Even if there is a chance for job security, many younger workers simply aren't interested in staying with one company for the promise of an eventual pension decades in the future. Their future success will come from their ability to be entrepreneurial.

Whether we blame it on lack of job security or the demise of company loyalty, the fact remains...it may be time to kiss Plan A goodbye.

Financial Security Is Still Possible

I attended a business presentation a few years ago with a US Census chart that illustrated in 1994 only five out of one hundred people in the United States achieved financial security, and only one of those enjoyed *total financial freedom* (defined as being able to do and have virtually anything you want, within reason.) That statistic seems to still be true today.

This book can guide you through considering—maybe for the first time—how to create your Plan B so you can become one of those enjoying total financial freedom.

Take a minute to step back and think about what your environment has taught you so far. The education system has been designed to move students into jobs working for someone else. A typical high school education does not teach the basics of business, nor does a two- or four-year degree. Master's degree programs train you to be even more valuable inside an organization but do not teach you to run your own company. My undergraduate business degree and two master's degrees certainly did not prepare me for the Plan B that I had to create. Traditional influences such as schools and family may have originally led you away from creating a Plan B and urged you toward getting a job.

Now, however, a Plan B is within your reach and you have the power to create one. Like anything else you have started, it will be a journey, but this time you will have a road map of what lies ahead.

How Did We Get Here?
(And where are we going?)

The details may be quite different, but the pattern is basically the same. We have made decisions that did not work out as we had planned. Additionally, local, national, and international economics have directly impacted each of us. How long it will take to recover from any losses will vary based on many things, such as the skills you have, your initiative, and the strength of the demand for what you can offer others.

The goal of this book is to help you make the best choices in these difficult times, and to give you a lot of insider information. You will learn the good, the bad, and the ugly about each of the Plan B options so you can choose yours wisely.

Clearly, I cannot know your specific goals for financial security and what you hope to be doing as you continue your work life. I can, however, show you useful, timely information so you can consider what might be possible.

Your grandparents could have lived quite well on $30,000 a year at retirement. Their mortgage was probably paid off and their lifestyle was simple. Vacations once a year were the norm. But today, the lifestyle expectations of those approaching retirement aren't about staying home and watching television. Instead, they are about travel-ing, volunteering, and remaining active. All of those ac-

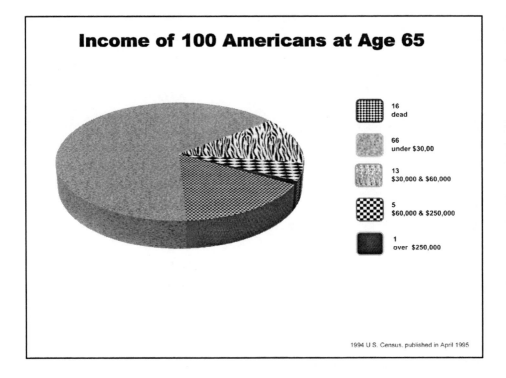

Income of 100 Americans at Age 65

16
dead

66
under $30,00

13
$30,000 & $60,000

5
$60,000 & $250,000

1
over $250,000

1994 U.S. Census, published in April 1995

tivities cost money. And your grandparents didn't have cell phone, internet access, or cable bills to pay either.

Statistically speaking, above are the data of the average income of people in the United States from 1996.[1]

Who Is Going to Pay the Bills When You Retire?

One of the early working titles of this book was, "What is your Plan B, or will you have to work until you die?" It was too long for a title, but it's still quite apt as a point to ponder.

Facing the facts, most of us are going to be on our own. Social Security is a mere pittance, if it even survives the next few decades. Pension plans are pretty much becoming a thing of the past. Research on the funding levels of some local and state retirement plans for government workers revealed many of them were well below the levels needed to deliver on the promises made. That means some retirement funds don't have enough money to pay for the employee pension and medical benefits costs that have been earned by workers, and those plans will eventually run out of money. For some people, the checks will simply stop coming.

One of the many reasons for the funding problems in both public and private sectors is that we are living longer. Life expectancy in 1950 was sixty-eight; in 2002 it jumped to seventy-seven. That means people are receiving pension payments, medical benefits, and social security checks almost a decade longer than our relatives did fifty years ago. Many more people are celebrating their one-hundredth birthday, and it takes a lot of money to live well for that long.

Companies, hit hard by the down economy, are scaling back. Of those that survive, many will no longer offer lifelong pensions or medical benefits. One Federal Bureau of Investigation (FBI) agent told me they have nicknamed their new pension plan "the work until you die plan." New hires at a variety of organizations are told they will not have medical benefits after they retire. Certainly AT&T, GM or Citibank aren't going to offer job security or guarantee a retirement plan. Even if they wanted to, they are not able to afford it.

We all want to hold on to the lifestyle that we've worked so hard to achieve. We don't want to shrink it, or live a narrower life. Yet, many people's dreams are melting down as the economic growth stalls. In-

> In 2000, there were approximately 68,000 people over 100 years of age in the United States. In 2050, the projected number is 834,000.
>
> —U.S. CENSUS

> Hallmark Cards sold approximately 85,000 "Happy 100th Birthday" cards in 2007.
>
> —WSJ BLOG, "HALLMARK'S CENSUS OF CENTENARIANS," APRIL 10, 2008

vestments have destroyed many retirements. *Poof!* It's gone. There may not be enough hours or days left to simply work longer and harder to replenish the retirement fund.

Financial advisors just a few years ago taught us the rule of thumb that we need 65% of our yearly income to keep our same lifestyle in retirement. Then the figure went to 80%. The percent that is the right number for you will, of course, depend on your expenses and lifestyle. Be sure to discuss this with your retirement experts to determine what your *happily ever after* number will be.

Social Security Benefits

When it was originally introduced, Social Security was designed to offer financial assistance to help the aging population survive. But that was back in 1935, when the average life expectancy was less than sixty-five years.

When Social Security payouts began, there were, on average, over forty workers paying into the fund and their monies supported one retiree—a ratio of more than 40 to 1. With the invention of the birth control pill and family planning tactics, our country's birth rate dropped. In 2000, for example, the ratio of workers to retirees was 3.4 to 1. By 2050, or when today's college students reach retirement age, the ratio will be 2 to 1. Many other developed nations face the same concern: not enough younger workers paying social security taxes to support the growing number of seniors.[1]

For decades, we've heard warnings that the Social Security fund will run out of money. The most recent projection is it will be totally depleted by the year 2036.[2]

Besides the increase in longevity and the decreased number of workers paying taxes per retiree, another contributing factor is the repeated withdrawals on Social Security funds to balance the federal budget or to pay for other government programs. Unfortunately, social security payments are the only income many retirees will receive, which will create extreme hardship when the fund dries up.

Retirement Plans Designed to Benefit... Whom?

Traditional jobs have created pensions designed to provide lifelong retirement income, even for those employees with as few as twenty years of service, regardless of the employee's age.

One example of this is the military—certainly a dangerous and demanding career. A common career choice is to join for twenty years, then retire and begin receiving a 50% pension payout right away. This is a sweet deal: join the military at age twenty, work for twenty years, retire at age forty, live until age one hundred, and enjoy a sixty-year pension payout which is three times longer than the time served in the military.

For example, one forty-something retired soldier shared with me that he retired after twenty years of service and is now receiving $31, 000 annually for the rest of his life. It is not enough to fund a great lifestyle, true, but it is a steady check.

> An Illinois highway maintenance worker can earn up to $148,000 annually with overtime. The state's enhanced early retirement program will pay that person up to $75,000 per year, starting at age fifty and after twenty-five years on the job. By age eighty, that person will have received $1.2 million more than a participant would have in the state's regular retirement plan.
>
> —*FLORIDA TODAY*, DECEMBER 9, 2011, "TAXPAYERS ARE LEFT WITH A TICKING TIME BOMB"

The problem is that no government or organization can sustain that kind of cash outlay for long.

Let's take a closer look at the types of pension plans that have been popular in recent decades, and why you can't count on them for retirement income. There are three primary types: defined benefits, defined contributions, and individual retirement accounts, or IRAs.

The traditional *defined benefit pension plan* guaranteed how much you would receive each month in retirement. The plan was designed to reward only those with lengthy employment for a predetermined number of years with one organization or government institution. Now, however, it has become too expensive and too difficult to fund this type of pension plan because people live longer and investments funds don't always grow fast enough. It is rare to find this kind of lucrative pension anymore; they typically are only offered by large, mature companies or by government organizations.

The next type of plan is the *defined contribution pension plan,* which is the direction many organizations have moved toward (and away from the defined benefits plans described above). In a defined contribution pension plan, the organization contributes a specific amount (the defined contribution) into a pension plan each month. An employee must stay with the company for a stated number of years in order to eventually receive the company's contribution. This is known as vesting.

For example, you may have to work for an organization for ten years to be fully vested in the plan. If they lay you off after nine years—too bad. Some or all of their contribution to your pension is gone. Any contribution you made to your retirement is still yours, but they get to keep theirs.

Or if the pension plan manager made some bad investment decisions, your entire pension may be gone. Or if the company becomes strapped for cash or files bankruptcy, your pension payout may be reduced or even gone. A friend of mine, married to an airline pilot for a major airline, said they had expected to enjoy a nice retirement lifestyle until the company cut her husband's pension payout by half. Instead of retiring, when he was forced to at age sixty-five, he had to scramble to find another job.

The last pension plan configuration, the *individual retirement account,* or *IRA,* is often called a 401(k) in the corporate world, a 403(b) for non-profits, and a 457 for government employees. In this plan, an employee contributes a percentage of his earnings before taxes to the plan, which means he pays less overall in income taxes. Some organizations will match this contribution up to a specific amount.

For example, for each dollar you contribute, the organization may add anywhere from three to fifty cents to your account. You're typically able to choose how the funds are invested from choices the company offers. Your contribution is always available to you, but their contribution is tied to a specified length of time you must work for them before you are vested in the plan. The plan is designed to allow you to move your pension funds with you if you change jobs. If you do that, you can move your IRA to your new organization and select from that company's investment options. Or you can move your IRA to an independent company that allows you to totally control your investments. Unfortunately this has been disastrous for many people, because they did not know how to make good investment decisions and have lost significant money they may never recover.

The balancing act for organizations on what they can provide is difficult. Regulation has become intense because of scandalous activities in the past, including the infamous ENRON, Arthur Andersen, WorldCom, Global Crossing, Adelphia Communications, and Tyco International. Plan administrators have to surround themselves with expert alternatives for their employees, so they stay compliant with the ever-changing regulations and laws.

Wrap Up

What the information in this chapter means to you is that if you know—or have a sneaking suspicion—that you are vulnerable to losing your Plan A job, you are one of the smart ones who are paying attention. You can create a better future for yourself and your family, and this book will show you how.

If you don't think you are vulnerable, you are someone I most want to reach, because it's easier to create a Plan B before you actually need one. And you will need one.

Each Plan B option explained in this book has specific advantages and disadvantages; I've presented them in such a way that you will be able to easily understand and mentally try them on for size. You will also learn the good and bad news about each option, which means you can eliminate the Plan B options that are not of interest or available to you. Thus, you can focus on those that match your needs and desires. You'll use your time and money in meaningful and productive ways.

In the next chapter, you will start your journey to determine the best Plan B match for you. The answers and *aha!* moments you gain from chapter 2 will help you evaluate each Plan B option to ensure it does match what you really want for yourself.

Specifically, you will identify:

- Your *why*—why you are creating a Plan B
- The *life values* that are most important to you
- What you *don't want* and *do want* in your life

Come with me to the next page...

Notes

1 Social Security Administration

Office of Research and Statistics, January 1996

Income of Population 55 or Older

1994 U.S. Bureau of the Census, April 1996

Chart from *System 7 – Five Point, One Team Global*

January 2010,

Melbourne Beach, FL

The wealthy 1% was not defined, but it was inferred to be $250,000.

2 Associated Press

"Social Security finances worsen,"

Florida Today, May 15, 2011

CHAPTER 2

Is Your *WHY* Bigger than Your *BUT?*

NOW YOU NEED THE STRUCTURE and the tools for working and thinking through what your Plan B could be like.

This chapter provides the framework for that, because here you will identify what you really want, so you can avoid those *"but...!"* blocks and be able to know—deep in your soul—the powerful *why* behind your need for a Plan B. Even better, you'll also see *why* you can confidently go forward with your very own personalized Plan B that you will create later in this book.

The information and exercises in this chapter are very important because, as you begin to identify and explore the Plan B ideas, you will have the foundation to conduct your own due diligence, ask the right questions, have the criteria to effectively analyze your options, and understand the consequences of your choices before you take action.

In a nutshell, you will have an *aha!* moment. You will know yourself and what you want, and your vision of the future—your *why*—will be clearer and thus more attainable.

All of this is designed to prevent you from making decisions and taking action that you might regret six months or a few years from now. You can avoid the same mistakes I made because I did not have these tools—the tools I eventually discovered or developed.

Here is Martha's Plan B *aha!* moment. Does it sound familiar? If not, it could!

> The monthly Human Resources meeting loomed near and Martha really didn't have the time to go, but the topic was just too timely: ***What is your new Plan B?*** She knew she needed one because her employer, a government agency, had already announced plans to cut the staff by half. On top of that, all employees had recently learned that they must actually reapply for their own jobs. No one was safe.
>
> Martha really wanted to keep working in this field, but she thought, "Maybe it is time for a Plan B." So she made the time to attend the meeting.
>
> I began the meeting with an exercise. It was designed to be extremely thought provoking. Interviewing a partner, attendees asked:
>
> • Tell me about a time you loved what you were doing.

- What do you value about yourself?
- What would you like to see your life like at retirement?

The third question got Martha's fire going as she vividly described what she wanted: "a two-bedroom, two-story house at the beach on the island where I grew up. The house faces the ocean with floor-to-ceiling windows." She could almost smell the salt in the air and feel the ocean breezes.

Then a cold reality crept in. "If I keep doing what I have been doing—taking care of others—I will never have my house on the beach. I need a Plan B now," she blurted in astonishment to her partner.

Martha had taken a crucial step by verbalizing her vision to another human being. She could feel the excitement take hold, and she could now clearly articulate her *why* for the change she knew she would have to make.

Your *why* is the reason you take action. It's the reason you are willing to move out of the protective cocoon you have been nestled in. Some of you are simply ready for a move and will be filled with feelings of adventure and excitement. Others will be kicking and screaming as they're forced to move because their life has been turned upside down by a layoff, illness, or personal loss. Their feelings will come from a sense of loss, which will, in turn, create feelings of denial, anger, regret, and fear. It is a normal, expected human reaction.

Your *why* will come from either moving toward something you want or running away from something you don't want. Emotions motivate us. Pain, unfortunately, is the most powerful motivator; it's five times more powerful than pleasure. Let's face it; sometimes the catalyst for running away can be pretty powerful.

There are three emotions that will help you create your *why:*

- Pain
- Fear
- Pleasure

In descending order, these emotions provide the power to motivate us:

1. <u>Pain in the present</u>. It is the most powerful driver of action. For example, your car quits and you have to buy a new one or you can't get to work. You take action now. Or, in a routine medical exam, you find out that you are pre-diabetic so you dramatically change what you eat, and you take more seriously the need to exercise and reduce stress.

2. <u>Fear is pain that is expected in the future</u>. It is strong, but not as strong as pain in the present. If fear is too overwhelming, you may feel paralyzed and not able to act. For example, pending layoffs create a lot of fear; you have a job for now but you know it's going away in the future. Some people will start job-hunting immediately; others will spend time complaining and blaming others for their pending doom.

3. <u>Pleasure in the present</u>. This, too, can be a motivator. Let's say it's a warm day so you decide to go hiking and enjoy the weather instead of finishing a report due tomorrow. Or, you have so much fun at a dinner party that you stay out longer than you had

planned, even though you have an important business meeting the next morning.

4. <u>Pleasure in the future</u>. This is the weakest motivator. For example, many people spend more time planning their vacations than ensuring they'll have a comfortable retirement. Or, on a more immediate level, you hang out on the couch and watch television instead of going to the gym, even though you want to look good in your new bathing suit when summer comes.

So what is the pain for you now? What are you afraid might happen? What feels good? What do you wish for? Each question brings new insight and answers to you.

Why is it important to you? What would your life be like if you had what you wished for? What will you have to change to create it? When you want something different in your life, it means that something has to change—including you—to get it. Are you willing to do what it takes?

When your *why* has real, emotional power over you, you will be willing to do whatever it takes.

Any change of great consequence requires a strong vision that will create a fire in your belly. This vision can be one that inspires you or scares you. And, although knowledge can be a powerful motivator, people aren't helped or changed simply by having more information. Real change happens when you are inspired. Inspiration comes when you have a created a powerful *why*.

Scarlett O'Hara's classic line in the movie *Gone with the Wind*, "I will never be hungry again," is the epitome of the perfect *why*. Like her, your *why* becomes the fuel for you to move outside your comfort zone. It is what you will need to remember to help keep you going, especially when you experience resistance, or things get hard, or those closest to you don't support you. Your *why* will shape the stories you tell yourself and others.

At first, your *why* may be a problem, a pain, or something that scares you. Mine certainly was. When it became clear the start-up company I had been working on with a partner stalled, it dawned on me I was in trouble. I had invested almost two years in working part-time on the new company, and I had let my consulting and coaching business dwindle. My money was running out. Then, as the economy collapsed, some of my investments didn't just drop in value—they were crushed. One investment just disappeared. *Poof!* It was gone. The pain and fear of running out of money was my motivation for change. I felt pretty stupid and scared. *Geez,* I thought, *I have three degrees and an impressive resume, but none of that matters now.* What did matter was what I was going to do about it.

No matter what your situation, your *why* must be bigger and more compelling than any excuse you can find for not pursuing your dream. Your *why* must be bigger than your *but.*

Determine Where You Are

Because you have read this far into the book, you are probably ready to move forward. I suspect you are looking at your life and reprioritizing it. That's good!

But before you figure out exactly where you want to go—and particularly how you'll get there—you need to identify where you are right now. The rest of this chapter will help you with this process by providing several tried-and-true tools. They will help you create clarity around what is working well in your life versus what needs your attention and some additional work. These tools will help you build your roadmap.

Determining What You Are Ready to Improve

> "It's not hard to make decisions when you know what your values are."
>
> — ROY DISNEY

Few people can compartmentalize their lives anymore, and there's no doubt your Plan B will involve your entire life—all aspects of it. The Life Values Model will help you determine where you are in eight key areas of your life. The model provides a chart that allows you to visualize aspects of your life that you are and are not satisfied with. It helps you decide what you want to improve or ignore as you create your Plan B. Again, you need a roadmap if you want to arrive at a specific destination, and

LIFE VALUES MODEL

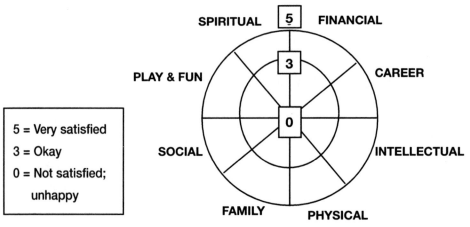

5 = Very satisfied
3 = Okay
0 = Not satisfied; unhappy

Source: Unknown

the Life Values Model is one of the first important tools to help you determine your path.

You will evaluate eight areas of your life, and you can specifically define what each one means to you. (You can also add a new area to the chart, if you wish, which means you'll have nine or more wedge-shaped sections instead of the eight shown here.)

Draw a line across each area to identify how satisfied you are in each of them (see examples in the next illustration). If you are really satisfied with an area, then you will draw a line close to the outside edge, in keeping with the number 5, or "very satisfied" outer section of each wedge. If you are not satisfied, or you are unhappy, then the line will be drawn closer to the middle, to zero.

When you have drawn your lines across each area, color them in, as shown in the example below.

Once you have colored in your model, look at it thoughtfully.

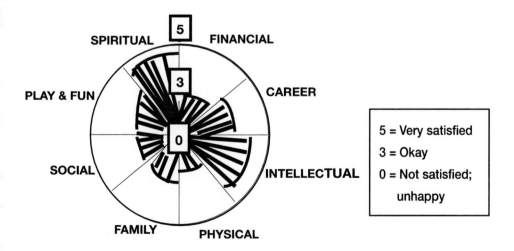

If you were to imagine your results as a wheel and roll it across the table, how smoothly would your chart roll? Ideally—and because you can define your own requirements for "satisfaction"—each aspect could eventually be fully satisfied creating a lifestyle that will roll smoothly on.

Do you want to change any of the areas that you are not satisfied with? If not, that's okay.

If you do want to improve your score in two or three values, which one do you want to work on first? To help you decide where to start, focus on the primary reason or reasons you want to create a Plan B. Money? New career? That's the one to focus on first. By doing so, you will create a *why* that's so compelling you will decide to do what it takes to create a Plan B. Your *why* will be bigger than your *but*.

Next, you will identify *why* you want to improve the area you have selected. For example, since this book is about helping you create a Plan B, then I believe you've probably rated the area of finance lower than you have the other wedge-shaped areas. Let's use this section as an example to define what it would take to later rate it as a four or five—to be very satisfied with the financial aspect of your life.

First, let's define what "very satisfied" would look like.

- *Definition:* I decide that being very satisfied in the financial area of my life includes an annual income of over $250,000. Within seven years, I will not need to actively work to create it; it will come to me through what I have created to that point. For example, the income will come from more books, events, and group and individual coaching programs that I will have created and implemented by the end of those seven years.

Second, let's look at *why* it is important for you. To do this, determine what you will have, be, and see when you feel very satisfied about this financial aspect. Describe what is happening in your life.

- *Why:* For me, satisfaction in the financial area includes having a nice home that is paid for, the ability to travel across the United States and the world, to be generous with my time and money so I can help others, to enjoy the luxuries of top-rated hotels, castles, and yachts in fabulous locations, to make a difference in people's lives, to have incredible experiences, and to study new things.

Next, let's begin to make it real. Create a description of what your life is like as if this very satisfied feeling has already happened, as if it exists for you right now.

- *Making it Real:* One example of a *why* in my financial section is to have a very nice home. Here's what I envision as I begin to make it real:

  ➢ I drive up to my large, two-story house with a big, wraparound porch and rocking chairs. The weather is warm and the humidity is comfortable. The neighborhood is filled with trees, and birds are singing nearby. Flowers bloom everywhere, and I can smell them as I walk in the front door. The kitchen is on the left, the patio is just outside the family room. Through the patio's glass doors, I can see the intercoastal waterway behind the house. Built to the highest green and energy-efficient standards; it boasts five bedrooms, two offices, and six bathrooms. The large kitchen has white cabinets and a free-standing island with a second sink. The island is raised on one side and is large enough to have five chairs pulled up to it. One wall in the kitchen is all glass; it faces out onto the garden, which is filled with vegetables, herbs, and fruit trees. There is also a greenhouse behind the garden. Because the house is located on water with ocean access, I see my nineteen-foot Flying Scot sailboat and my forty-one-foot Sea Ray Sundancer powerboat tied to my dock. I smile as I remember everything is paid for; there are no loans or mortgages.

When you make it real, be sure to engage all of your senses—see it in 3D. Put on some music that gets you revved up and excited about the future you can create for yourself.

Here are some questions to help get you started:

- What does it look like, as you see it in your mind's eye?
- What sounds do you hear as you experience it?
- What does it feel like—the temperature, the textures?
- What does it smell like?
- If someone wrote an article about it, what would it say?

Imagine how much fun you can have as you imagine what it would look and feel like to be very satisfied with the area in your life that you have selected to improve.

You are imagining what it would be like to live large; doing, having, and feeling everything you want.

Right now, your job is to daydream. Relax, and just be in the now. This process could take you a few minutes or maybe even a few hours. Or maybe you want to try several ideas on for size, so you'll do this exercise over several days. Think big. It's yours alone to decide and create, so be bold.

This will help you create a clear *why* for yourself. A jigsaw puzzle is easier to put together when you have the box with the picture on it, just like a roadmap helps you arrive more efficiently at your destination.

Also, putting your ideas down on paper in black and white is more powerful than just thinking or talking about them. When you see it in writing—or maybe you decide to draw pictures instead—you will see your ideas in different ways, and you will gain new insights as you look at the total picture.

Creating your *why* is an organic process. It will grow, shift, and become more powerful as you work with it and develop it. Your *why* may come quickly to you; other people may take a little longer to create theirs.

Remember, the clearer you become, the faster the universe can help you create it.

Identifying What You *Don't Want* and *Do Want*

The next step in creating your powerful *why* is to determine what you don't and do want in life. It is important because it will help you move in the direction you want to go—not where others think you should go. Now is not the time to "should" on yourself. When I created my list, I found it was easier to identify what I didn't want than to identify what I did want. You may too, but let's not waste time wondering about it.

Get out a piece of paper or hop on your computer and begin to list what you don't want in your life or your future.

For each **Don't Want** statement, create one or more **Do Want** statements. Identify what you wish you would be able to create, so you can make your list positive-sounding and so it can overcome all your negatives. This is an important step—seeing the flip side of what you don't want. Again, like a jigsaw puzzle, it is easier if you defined the edges first.

I had a powerful *why* for change. I knew I did not want to *have* to work until I died. I did not want to work seven days a week, barely able to squeeze in church services (during which I obsessed about work and only pretended to listen anyway).

I wanted a sense of ease about money. I wanted the time and money to travel to beautiful places and linger as long as I want. (Isn't it interesting that when we have the time, we don't have the money? Or when we have the money, we don't have the time? Or does this just happen to me?)

Use my list as an example for your own.

A List of *Don't Want* and *Do Want* Examples

Don't Want	Do Want
Worry that when I stop working, there will be no money coming in	Money that comes in whether I am working or not
	A sense of ease that my money and income are safe
	To be able to invest in people and programs that will give them a 'hand up' for success
	Financial freedom to afford just about anything I want
To be a workaholic, working six to seven days a week	Time to play, travel, and relax; time to truly live life
	Time to exercise regularly each week
	Freedom to choose how I want to spend my time each day
Only a few friendships because I have no time to invest in developing them	To develop more friendships with smart, funny people who support my interests and can travel with me
	To have a small and diverse group of friends with whom I can share ideas and have fun

You can see how creating contrasting statements about what you don't and what you do want can create clarity faster for you. Most people are very clear about what they don't want (complaining and blaming) but have not focused on what they do want instead. This process helps you identify what you are moving away from and, more importantly, what you are moving toward. The pain of what you are moving away from can help you create your powerful *why,* but your focus must be on what you *do* want because you will naturally move in the direction of your focus.

My *why* is powerful in keeping me motivated to park myself in a chair on weekends and early in the morning to write this book, to find and interview successful people, and to locate opportunities to speak to groups about how to create their Plan B. What have you identified so far as your *why?* A powerful vision will bring joy and pleasure to your mind and your heart. You must be leaning forward and into the future to create what you want.

As a fun example of the need to create and keep a powerful vision of where you want to go, let me share a story told by Tony Robbins, a well-known transformational coach and personal-growth guru. Tony's insight came from learning to drive a high-speed race car. He talked about how, as the car accelerated going into the racetrack turn, it started sliding sideways and toward a large, solid-concrete wall. Using big gestures, he made sure we saw the same thing he did:

> The wall had paint streaks on it from cars that had already sideswiped it. Like most of us would probably do, Tony stared at the wall as it came closer and closer.
>
> His instructor reached over, grabbed his head, and snapped it back to face the direction they needed to go. The instructor reminded him to

focus on where they were going and not on the wall. Tony said that he heard what the instructor said, but turned his head back to stare at the fast-approaching wall. The instructor again grabbed Tony's head and told him to look where they needed to go down the track, and not to let up on the accelerator. With high drama, Tony talked about how, out of the corner of his eye, he saw the wall continuing to come closer and closer.

Finally, the wheels got traction and the car swerved toward the straightaway, leaving the wall behind, because Tony was facing down the track, where they needed to go, and not looking directly at the wall, where he didn't want to do.

The point of the story is that if Tony had continued to stare at the wall, that is where he and the instructor would have ended up. But by focusing on where they needed to go, the car responded, and they headed for the finish line. You must have a clear vision of where you want to go, not where you have been or where you don't want to go.

What You Have Created So Far

You have started to create your powerful *why* by identifying what you want to change. Using your Life Values Model, you rated your level of satisfaction in eight different areas. You picked one or two areas in which you want to improve, and you defined what it would mean to increase your level of satisfaction with it. I hope you also had fun as you described the future you want— what it would look like, sound like, feel like, and even smell like.

You continued forming your *why* when you listed what you don't want and what you do want for your future. This helped you gain clarity in what you will be moving toward as you create your Plan B.

The work you have done is critical. Getting started on your Plan B will take a lot more work and effort, but you've already taken the first and very important steps. For example, consider that most of the fuel needed to launch rockets into space is burned in the first few minutes so the rocket can escape the earth's gravitational pull. Since I live just thirteen miles from the Kennedy Space Center, I have watched numerous space shuttle and rocket launches. Within a few minutes of launch, I see light reflecting off of the empty rocket-fuel boosters after they are used up and fall into the Atlantic Ocean. Once the rocket or shuttle has reached orbit, it needs very little fuel to sustain its journey.

Thus, creating what you want will require a lot from you in the beginning, but it will be much easier once you reach your orbit. Launching your rocket will likely require more personal work—on yourself. (Yes, I hate this part and you may too.) I know very few people who feel confident when they try something new, or who already have a strong, unshakeable sense of self esteem. You will be building new skills, developing new habits, and learning more so that you can create something different in your life and your future.

Since this is about creating your Plan B and how to jump-start your next career, the focus of this book is on creating an income that you will find satisfying and profitable based on what you want and like. We will focus on everything you bring to the table—your skills, your experience, and your preferences.

Once upon a time, we could separate work from our personal lives. We could take real vacations without staying connected to the office. Now, it's rare to be able to do that, so you might as well do what you like and are good at.

As you look at your answers to questions and assignments in this chapter, you should be very pleased with yourself. Each step moves you toward the future you want with a clear and powerful *why* so you will do what it takes to create your Plan B.

As you read the rest of this book, use what you have learned about yourself in this chapter as a way to *feel* if the options are a good match for you. Richard Branson, chairman of Virgin Group, Ltd., shared in an interview that when he considers new ideas, he gathers and reads all of the data and research available. Then he makes his decision with his gut. Some decisions have been wrong but a lot more of them have been right. Not bad for a guy who has created a multi-billion-dollar empire and runs it from wherever in the world he wants to be, including his own island in the Caribbean.

Wrap Up

You have learned a lot about yourself, what you want to create, and what you want your life to be like. You will use the answers you have found in this chapter over and over to help evaluate the ideas and options you discover in this book and on your journey to create a Plan B. So if you skipped over the exercises, you are on the ski lift without your skis. Go back and do the work because you will need the skis for the fast track you are on.

Your answers from this chapter will give you a structure to quickly say yes or no, so you don't waste time or money on something that is not right for you. This is especially helpful if you are distracted by "bright and shiny" objects or ideas. Your answers will also help you determine if an idea or option will take you closer or farther away from what you want.

Your answers are powerful tools.

In the next chapter, you will learn more about what awaits you as you create your Plan B. You will read about one woman's journey to create her Plan B cupcake empire; what she learned can help you too.

Each chapter in this book teaches you what might normally take you years to figure out. I know, because that's how long it's taken me to find out this really exciting stuff—and some of the insider information you may not have ever been able to find. Just think about how much faster you can go and farther along you will be when you use this book and its tools as your roadmap.

Get ready for more discoveries ahead…

CHAPTER 3

The Real Deal about You

AN APPRECIATION OF THE SKILLS I already had and a realization of those that I would need to find or develop are two of the gifts I received as I worked on my Plan B and this book. You too will come to recognize the many ways in which you are growing as a person as you become more successful with your Plan B.

This chapter continues the journey you started in chapter 2. Here, you will learn important, useful information, such as what your Plan B journey may look like, an example of the key traits of serial entrepreneurs, the five requirements of successful change, and how to find and listen to the right people.

I have been on a lifelong journey of change and learning, and I have grown and can play at a higher level than someone who is just starting out on a journey of personal development. I am a professed self-improvement junkie—and, yes literally walked through fire—on purpose—as a personal growth exercise.

Here is another example of an experience that helped me realize that if I'm going to have the life I want, I would have to start making different choices and taking different actions. It helped me remember how critical it was to keep doing my personal work if I wanted more for me in life.

I was standing in a darkened room in a Denver convention center with several thousand other people. Tony Robbins was nearing the climax of what he calls the Dickens Process (because it mirrors the script of *A Christmas Carol,* with the ghosts of the past, the present, and the future). He had led us to the point where each of us was face to face with our past and present failures. The room was filled with heartfelt sobs and heavy sighs. Just like the ghosts had led the character of Scrooge to see the misery he had created for himself, Tony's words dredged up our buried failures for us to confront.

> His voice boomed over the speakers as he told us, "You have exactly what you want in your life: the relationships, the money, the lifestyle. You have created it all." The sobbing grew louder as he commanded us to think back over all of our failed relationships—we are the only common denominator.

> "If you want something different," he reminded us, "you must *do* something different. Where will you be in six months if you keep doing what you are doing now? One year? Five years? Ten years? How does it feel to keep doing what you have been doing?"

Loud screams and moans of agony surrounded me; tears were streaming down my face. The pain of sadness and frustration stabbed me deeply. Many despairing people grabbed their belongings and ran for the doors, only to find their way blocked by Tony's event staff, trained to keep them in the room and in the moment. He asked those people trying to exit, "What else in your life have you just run away from?"

Tony was relentless. He demanded we each identify one thing that we must change. He assured us we already knew what it was. Our job was to just say it aloud—yell it at the top of our lungs, in fact.

"Shout it now," he ordered us.

The yells were deafening.

Tony was right...I did know what I needed to do, and it would not be easy or quick. I would have to make different choices, take different action, and find others who could help me. After all, it really is my choice to stay stuck or to move forward.

I decided to move forward, not really sure what it would look like. But it's like what Steve Jobs often said in the early days of Apple Computer, "It's all about the journey."

Now, you are about to be introduced to the hero's journey, a classic literary device for constructing a story. After all, you have already started a journey of your own. So let's see what might lie ahead of you and what you can learn from reading about one woman's successful hero's journey.

The Hero's Journey

How many times have you noticed that a lot of TV shows and movies are so predictable that you know what's going to happen before the plot unfolds? The main character struggles but somehow he or she rises to the top, fights off all the bad guys, and either lives happily ever after or is ready for the next adventure.

These stories are familiar and predictable because they typically follow a pattern known as the *hero's journey*, a phrase coined by mythology expert Joseph Campbell. According to Campbell, all myths are based on the same idea. The hero undertakes a journey or adventure of some type. You can find modern examples of the hero's journey in such movies as *Star Wars* and *Avatar*. The Harry Potter books all follow this classic pattern.

When you embark on a Plan B, you are off on your own form of a hero's journey. To achieve success (i.e., complete the journey), you will move through a number of identifiable phases. Campbell described fifteen different events or phases in the classic hero's journey, most of which you will likely experience.

I have grouped the concepts into three segments—Departure, Initiation, and Return—that will encompass Campbell's fifteen phases.

Departure

A departure is a beginning, just like when you depart from the airport on a flight out of town. We all start somewhere. Maybe this is a conscious choice we make.

Or maybe the departure is forced on us by circumstances of life.

We've all had friends who were laid off from jobs and yet managed to land on their feet; they wound up more successful than they'd ever been before. They departed from their old line of work or job only because they were forced to, but they moved into a new, more profitable and personally satisfying one. For many of them, it was the best thing that ever happened to them.

> A journey of 1000 miles begins with a single step.
> —CHINESE PROVERB

The fact that you picked up this book tells me it's probably time for your departure, even if you might not realize it yet. Perhaps you are paralyzed by the fear. It's normal to fear the unknown. (And it makes for great entertainment in books, movies, and on television.)

Change can be scary.

But go ahead anyway. Dip your toes into the water or just take the plunge. You need to do what you feel is best for you—not what you feel that others expect of you.

There will be no journey unless you depart.

Initiation

First you must be initiated.

The word *initiation* might make you think of hazing or some arduous task you must complete to prove yourself worthy of induction into a club or organization. That's not a bad way to think of it for this purpose. One phase of the Initiation segment of the hero's journey is often called *the road of trials.*

We've all heard of trials and tribulations, and we all go through them. They may seem awful at the time, but keep in mind that creating anything new takes time and effort to pay off in the future—few worthwhile successes are easy.

The friends who got laid off but wound up finding better, more profitable jobs didn't sit around eating chocolates while waiting for offers from CEOs beating down their front doors. That isn't how things happen. They had to get off the couch, update their résumés, take a few classes, and find work. They had to hustle.

> Luck is the place where preparation and opportunity cross.
> —COMMON ADAGE

Often we become so jealous of others, and we are so busy envying their good luck that we forget that successful people really do work for what they have. If you've decided to depart from one phase of your life, expect an initiation into the next phase—it might be a bit of a bumpy ride at first, but it'll be a path worth taking.

Return

In fairy tales, the characters live happily ever after. In westerns, they ride off into the sunset. In real life, however, heroes return to a new reality, and hopefully one that is better because of their efforts on their journey.

Once you depart or step away from something that needs changing, you are on your way to becoming someone different. You are being upgraded—as you journey through the Initiation segment. At first you will feel different—almost like you are not yourself—as you grow and learn.

You will, however, eventually return to feeling like yourself again. You might have more money, a better house, or a better job, but you're still you. For example, you may have studied hard and earned an important certification, getting recognition for top scores. You had to challenge yourself to keep focused to earn it, but after all of the excitement dies down you are still you, just smarter and more skilled.

The key here is to appreciate your struggles, because what you will go through will make you wiser and stronger. You will be at higher level because of what you have learned and done. Obstacles that, in the past, you would have found insurmountable will now be easier for you to conquer.

Below are some "sound bites" that would be typical of what you might find along the way on your hero's journey—the challenges and the triumphs. I've included mini-examples to help illustrate the various steps.

THE HERO'S JOURNEY
(The path to your Plan B)

DEPARTURE
(The first step, i.e., expressing a desire for change)

Call to Adventure: Passions, dreams, or disasters.

Refusal of the Call: Is it possible? No, I can't do it.

Supernatural Aid: "Use the Force, Luke." —OBI-WAN KENOBI, *STAR WARS*

Cross the Threshold: Explore options. You bought this book, right?

Belly of the Whale: Business plans, raising funds, intellectual properties.

INITIATION
(Paying your dues to join the club)
Road of Trials: Building the team.
Striving for profitability.
Meet the Goddess: Your first real customers.
Temptation: Shifting marketplaces.
Distractions, shiny things.
Atone before the Gods: Find your niche
among the competition.
Receive the Gift: Realize your new
business skills.

RETURN
("There's no place like home."—DOROTHY, *THE WIZARD OF OZ*)
Refusal to Return: Don't lose sight of the
core business.
The Magic Flight: Do you have an exit
strategy? IPO? Selling the company?
The Return Threshold: You are a success.
Master of Two Worlds: You have learned
what it takes to win.
Freedom to Live: Financial, time, and
personal freedom.

You can be confident that your journey will share some—maybe not all—of the same steps.

Here is a real-life example of the four-year hero's journey one woman has taken to date as she creates her new Plan B:

Holly Wilder, a striking, dynamic blonde with clear blue eyes, and a vivacious personality, was a celebrity chef in Hollywood. She cooked for Tom Cruise and Nicole Kidman, and made Christmas dinners for Jay Leno, to name a few. She also replaced the traditional craft service caterer on the television sets filming *Will and Grace, Seinfeld,* and *3rd Rock from the Sun* by creating a sit-down, fine-dining experience. Holly used fresh products to make delicious meals on the set, replacing the usual microwave, grab-and-go, fast-food tradition.

Although she was successful, she wanted to see what else she could create and what the marketplace would want.

Holly had *heard the Call,* the first step in the *Departure* segment of her hero's journey. As she began to think about her Plan B options, she realized she was not entirely clear on what she should do next. "Instead of a plan, it was more of an organic process," she told me. She knew for certain, however, that she wanted to develop a business that would leverage her cooking expertise.

As she researched trends to help her determine what would fit her needs, she found that cupcakes were hot products in New York and California but they had not yet found their way to the Southeast. Using that information, Holly developed a business concept combining cupcakes and tart frozen yogurt; one up-and-coming trend that could be duplicated. She was over the threshold and had *Departed* on her journey.

Holly's husband, Barry, is a seasoned professional in commercial real estate development, so she used his expertise to help select a location that was a "destination" and that offered a lot of business sales opportunities. As a result of his search, Holly and her family moved to Orlando in 2004.

Next, she picked the right store location. She needed one with a population density large enough to give her the walk-in traffic she needed to be successful. Waterford Lakes Town Center was the answer because it is one of the highest-targeted destinations (for shoppers) in the country. Thousands of cars come into the parking lot daily. She knew this location would regularly give her the appropriate density of foot traffic.

"We needed density like LA and New York have, with 100,000 people walking around. Orlando's population density is either at resorts or at Waterford Lakes Town Center. We were very specific when we selected the location to open the first store," Holly said.

She also wanted to look like a big, successful company even though she was starting with just one store; the Town Center again met her needs. The prestige location has big box stores (such as Target, Old Navy, and Victoria's Secret), with boutiques shops nestled in between them, ample convenient access, and significant walk-in traffic.

In 2008, Holly finally opened her first dessert destination, Sweet! By Good Golly Miss Holly.[1]

Her brand is big and visible, and one that includes a pink, refrigerator truck sporting her face on the back. It creates a visual splash as it drives through Orlando traffic to make deliveries. She knew her brand's success was critical and she was determined to make it work.

Her *Initiation* was a far cry from her Hollywood past, when she cooked for and served the celebrities. They knew they could depend on her to not be "one more thing they had to worry about" when she arrived to serve at their events. Her new business, on the other hand, had a grinding daily routine that included getting up at 3 a.m. and stuffing her long blonde hair under a hairnet to start baking that day's cupcakes.

Instead of paying a public relations firm to get the word out, Holly personally met with CEOs and top buyers to further emphasize that she was the face and the brand of her business. Because she likes to give back to the community that supports her, she offered cupcakes to the not-for-profit organizations within Florida. If they wanted 1,000 logoed or photograph cupcakes, she delivered them. She gave away over $100,000 worth of product to get her cupcakes into the right hands, which helped persuade them to place an order with her for their upcoming events.

Holly created one of her standard products— the mini-cupcake—by accident. A spa had ordered 500 smaller-than-normal cupcakes for its grand opening, but the night before the event, the spa's building burned to the ground. So, as any good businesswoman would do, she put them in her store's case and started selling them. She also realized their profitability when she sold four for $6.00, instead of one traditional (and larger) cupcake for $2.50. Her average sale went from $3.00 to $11.00. Today, the mini-cupcake is 80% of her sales.

To increase sales on Mondays—the slowest day of the week for eateries—Holly lowered the price of the mini-cupcakes from $1.50 to $1.00 and called it Mini Mania Monday. She created loyalty programs to give customers discounts and a reason to come back; she also made it possible to package and ship orders for next-day delivery. She remodeled the store and moved the frozen yogurt machine out from behind the counter to become self-service. She listened, learned, and innovated to find her niche in the marketplace, a.k.a., the *Atoning before the Gods* step in the *Initiation* segment.

After a year and a half of working eighteen-hour days, she realized she couldn't be in a hairnet, in the kitchen, and still build the business the way she needed to—she had to get out there. She was the face of the business. To make the shift, she had to learn to let go, which is very tough for perfectionist chefs in the kitchen. She stopped micromanaging her employees and instead let them do what they did best. Her management style shifted to making sure her employees knew the results she expected and then letting them make it happen. She had *Received the Gift* of business acumen and had learned new skills.

Then one day her children asked, "What is more important to you: us or your cupcakes?" Holly took this as the call to *Return*. She was a success. In three years, she had created and systemized the company and was ready to take it to the next level, but her dilemma was how to do it. She had already learned how to move out of the kitchen, and now her children had spoken. What next?

The answer came when the Food Network TV Channel found her in a Google search and called her. They were casting for a new show, *Cupcake Wars*. She sent in her audition tape, was selected, and flew back to Los Angeles to tape the shows. This was the *Magic Flight* in her *Return* segment of her hero's journey.

Holly's journey led her from Los Angeles to Orlando and back to Los Angeles. She went from cooking for celebrities to becoming a celebrity herself when she created the Savory Salmon Cupcake that led to her first win. She went from being a 3 a.m. batch baker to being a two-time winner on a popular cable television show.

After the big win, Holly looked up at the sky and wondered, "What can top this?" The answer came with a call from Abrams Books, a publisher who signed her to write a cookbook expected out in the spring of 2013. It will include one hundred savory recipes that can all be prepared in a classic American cupcake pan.

As I interviewed Holly about her cookbook, I asked her why she thought the cookbook would be successful, she said:

> "I am re-creating the breakfast, lunch, dinner, and snack preparation experience that can all be done in a cupcake pan. That means I am creating and testing each one of the one hundred recipes. It is exhilarating because I can offer a new, fun way to look at preparing food. And it's exhausting because the quality has to be perfect for each recipe every time. The cookbook can make people's lives easier."

Holly also told me that she finds it amusing that she had to move to Orlando to be discovered by Hollywood.

Here are a few other things she learned that can help you too:

- If you can't figure out how to make something happen, find someone who can.
- Create thoughtful products (her cupcakes are heart healthy).
- Much of your work will be an inside job (i.e., your personal growth) that starts by you claiming your success and knowing you deserve it. (Good news… you have already started this work in chapter 2.)

Where are you on your hero's journey? Because you are considering your Plan B, you have, at the very least, been *Called to an Adventure.* Use the concept of the hero's journey to give you a way to determine your progress and help you realize what might lie ahead. Your journey will begin in your mind and then it should capture your heart, for you will need both to keep on your path. Continually ask yourself this question, "What must I do, or do differently, or stop doing if the future is to be different from the past or present?"

The problem for many people is that they get in their own way. They procrastinate, blame others, have a string of excuses for failure, don't deliver promised results, or disappear emotionally or even physically. Heroes don't do that. They shed their constraints and put on their capes—and you can too.

Keep reading to discover the hero you must become to be successful with your chosen Plan B.

> Continually ask yourself this question, "What must I do, or do differently, or stop doing if the future is to be different from the past or present?"
>
> —KATHLEEN RICH-NEW, BUSINESS CONSULTANT, SPEAKER, EXECUTIVE COACH, CLARITY WORKS CONSULTING; AUTHOR, PLAN B

It Doesn't Take a Rocket Scientist to Launch a Plan B

To launch your Plan B successfully, you will need to learn new things, but don't worry—we are not talking about earning a PhD. You are already learning what you need to do because you are obviously ready and willing to think more deeply about what you want to create. You will notice you become a better you on your journey. The good news is you have a lot of what you need already within your reach, such as your own pool of experience, your network of resources, your knack of doing certain things well, and your vision of where you want to go.

The bad news is you probably don't have everything you will need. Consequently, you will have to find and build the rest of your resources to launch your Plan B. But you can do it, especially if your *why* is bigger than your *but*.

For example, if your background is that of an employee with a typical job, then you may not have developed your skills in such areas as managing projects or people, hiring and retaining staff, sales and marketing, or tracking cash flow. In a typical job, you are hired for a specific skill set and asked to do only a few things well.

Before your Plan B launch, you will need to identify your strengths so you can bring in others to compensate for your lack of skills in certain areas. Each area of expertise has its own learning curve. You don't need to become an expert but you should understand enough to know what to expect and how to direct others.

It always helps to study those who are successful and find out what makes them tick. Research by TTI Performance Systems, Ltd.,[2] on what they called *serial entrepreneurs* (defined as those who have created more than one successful business which employs others) showed that these entrepreneurs have similar traits:

- They have typically experienced success and usually failure too.
- They tend to learn from both, developing the professional skills vital for success.
- They have personal funds from previous ventures or have the ability to raise funds based on past successes.

The following chart uses the research to compare the rating of the serial entrepreneurs to the US adult mean in three key traits. Keep in mind this research is on people who have started several companies; you may be interested in starting only one.

Key Traits	Serial Entrepreneurs	US Adult Mean
Very Competitive	33%	12%
Rule Breaker	22%	12%
Quick to Change	7%	1%

TTI Performance Systems, Ltd [2]

VERY COMPETITIVE. Serial entrepreneurs are almost three times more *competitive* than the US adult mean. Once they have created more than one successful company, they fall in love with the thrill of building new companies, which also means they typically aren't interested in staying around once it moves into the maintenance mode. The competitive approach also means they have a will to win in every situation.

BREAK THE RULES. They are twice as likely to *break rules* to achieve goals as ordinary people. This can also be described as disrupting the established way of doing business. Consider the new ideas that are rampant in our world today that are going beyond the norm. College classes are offered online, which allows students access to top schools regardless of where they live. Two-year community colleges are offering four-year bachelor degrees. Electronic book readers allow instant access to thousands of e-books via downloads. Online bookstores offer unlimited shelf space to authors, since all these stores need is a warehouse or two, whereas brick-and-mortar bookstores are closing in record numbers. Prescription drugs are less expensive in Canada and Mexico, and trips over the borders are brisk. Wine has been repackaged from bottles with corks to boxes with built-in taps. Breaking the rules has been a way of business in our country for centuries; Americans focus on how to get product to customers faster, easier, and cheaper than competitors (domestic or international) can. Successful companies focus on what problems they can fix that people are ready to spend money on.

FASTER TO CHANGE. The third key trait, *faster to change,* is seven times higher in serial entrepreneurs than in the average US adult. Their goal is to achieve their vision and if they have to change their plans, they do it quickly. Amazon started as an online bookstore and now sells electronics, computers, clothes, automobile parts, and a long list of other items. They had to change their focus to continue to be successful and were willing to do so.

The research also identified the primary *values* of various types of serial entrepreneurs. Values motivate us to take action. Think about them as being equivalent to the air you breathe, the water you drink, and the food you eat. To survive, you must have air, water, and food or you will die. In this case, if your values are not being met, it may feel like you are dying.

Using the same research study from TTI, here is how the top three values of serial entrepreneurs compare to the average US adult.

Values	Serial Entrepreneurs	US Adult Mean
Utilitarian	62%	38%
Theoretical	21%	15%
Individual-istic	10%	9%

TTI Performance Systems, Ltd [2]

UTILITARIAN. The No. 1 value of serial entrepreneurs shows they want to get a return on their investment of time, energy and/or money. They are practical and want to discover what is useful in all areas of their life. Utilitarians work hard and expect to be rewarded for it.

Serial entrepreneurs are one and a half times more likely to be *utilitarian* than the mean number of US adults.

How dissatisfied you rated yourself in the financial and career area of the Life Values Model in chapter 2 is an indication of how important this value is to you.

This value also complements the key traits mentioned above: being very competitive, a rule breaker, and quick to change.

THEORETICAL. This second value focuses on finding the truth, gathering knowledge, solving problems, and using cold, hard facts and research. People with a strong theoretical value are good at solving problems; they're also objective in all areas and are skilled at identifying, differentiating, generalizing, and systematizing. Their basic attitude is they want to understand, discover, and systemize the truth. They feel compelled to learn and grow. If they are working in an area that is easily learned, they lose energy, go flat, and become bored.

Serial entrepreneur theoretical scores are almost one and a half times higher when compared with the US adult mean.

How "dissatisfied" you rated yourself in the intellectual area of the Life Values Model in chapter 2 is an indication of how important this value is to you. The more dissatisfied you were, the more importance you place on theoretical value.

INDIVIDUALISTIC. The third-highest value of these serial entrepreneurs is to increase power and advance their own personal position or that of their company's. They are good at leading, forming useful strategic alliances, and planning and carrying out a winning strategy. Their basic attitude is to assert themselves enough so their cause is victorious. They must advance themselves and/or their company.

The value of being individualistic is only a little higher—by 1%—in serial entrepreneurs than in the US adult mean. Interestingly, this difference is not nearly as dramatic as those differences in the first two values, so maybe that says something about the United States as a country: anyone can grow up to be president or start a business and become wealthy.

The financial and career areas in your Life Values Model are the most closely related to this value. How dissatisfied you rated yourself in the areas of finance and career are an indication of how important this value is to you.

Five Requirements for Successful Change

As we said at the beginning of this chapter, one of the benefits of working on a Plan B is realizing how much you will grow and improve yourself. No one shows up perfectly ready for what is coming next; your shortcomings will become crystal clear and point you to what you need to work on. The choice will be yours to adapt, make no changes, or find others who can do what you can't or won't.

Since Plan B is a journey, it's time to understand what you will need in order to create change. For example, how many times have you tried to change a simple habit and yet, after a short time, you went right back to doing the same thing? Has your organization ever announced a big change, only to have it fall flat on its face? Change rarely works as anticipated for a variety of reasons, including the failure to plan for and address all of the factors that are critical to implementing the desired changes.

This is a handy chart that helps distinguish each aspect you must address to create your Plan B. If any of the five aspects described are missing (as shown with the gray boxes labeled "Missing"), then feelings will likely arise that range from confusion to frustration over false starts.

FIVE REQUIREMENTS OF SUCCESSFUL CHANGE   **Results or Emotions**

Vision +	Skills +	Incentives +	Resources +	Action Plan =	Change
Missing	Skills +	Incentives +	Resources +	Action Plan =	Confusion
Vision +	Missing	Incentives +	Resources +	Action Plan =	Anxiety
Vision +	Skills +	Missing	Resources +	Action Plan =	Fragmented Change
Vision +	Skills +	Incentives +	Missing	Action Plan =	Frustration
Vision +	Skills +	Incentives +	Resources +	Missing	False Starts

Ambrose, D. (1987), "Managing Complex Change." Pittsburgh, PA: Enterprise Group

Let's look at each of the five aspects that are critical to successfully implementing change.

Vision

Your vision is the core of your Plan B. It's what you are creating, buying and/or building. It will require a long-term perspective because it takes time to move from where you are now to where you want to be. If you and your team do not all share the same strong vision, *confusion* on where you are going and what needs to be done will reign. In chapter 2, you already began creating your vision when you determined what you don't and do want for your life. Vision is the picture on your jigsaw puzzle box that allows you to see through the chaos and stay focused on where you are going.

Skills

Your current skills will get you part of the way to your successful Plan B. The question you must answer is what new skills do you need to develop and which are the ones you simply can't develop. For example, you may be brilliant with numbers and yet be a flop with managing people. Or you may be very creative but can't balance your checkbook. You cannot be all things to all people; you have been born with a specific set of skills and abilities that are hardwired from birth. You will need others to bring the skills you do not have. If you do not have the needed skills, then you and your team will feel *anxious*. That will tell you that you have to find someone who has what you are missing.

Incentives

The incentives represent what you and others on your team need so that everyone is focused on the same end-goal and will do what is required. Examples of incentives are achieving a mission or pursuing a passion, or gaining status, prestige, influence, or helping others. Incentives may or may not include money. If incentives are missing, you will have *fragmented change*. The *why* you developed in chapter 2 is your incentive and it must be bigger than your challenges (your *buts*).

Resources

Examples of the resources you will likely need to achieve your Plan B include cash, skills, staff, equipment, production, technology, processes, marketing, sales, delivery, and accounting. If you don't have the resources you need, you'll feel *frustrated*.

Action Plan

The last component is your action plan: what you need to do and how you will do it. What does this look like? This means a properly sequenced, well-executed, step-by-step plan. The action plan is your map to implementing everything you need to accomplish. You will also want short-, medium-, and long-range plans. For example, your long-range action plan may be to have thirty stores in the Southeast within ten years. The medium-range plan may be to open your first two stores locally within two years. The short-term goal is to identify the location for your first store. There are numerous resources already available to help you create your action plan, such as project-management training and software. If you don't have an action plan, then you will have *false starts*.

You may already know what help you will need, and you may be thinking about new ideas and different options. Perhaps you're already talking with others—your family, friends or associates—about your Plan B. The trick is to talk with people *who will be able to help you on your journey*...Where is Obi-Wan Kenobi when you need him?

Luke & Associates, a contract service provider, is a great example of what happens when the right team and the right plan come together and remain dedicated to the vision. The company was No. 3 on *Inc. Magazine's* 2011 List of 500 Fastest-Growing Companies. Luke started in 2006 with twenty employees and in 2011 they were projected to have grown to over 1,300 employees and revenues of $100 million, largely due to the $3 billion in government contracts for medical services they now have with the Armed Services. [3]

The company's start-up is even more impressive: three men, all working their Plan A jobs, got together and decided to create a Plan B, which became Luke & Associates. Each man had his own area of expertise: operations, information technology (IT), or government contracts. They worked their Plan B at nights and on weekends, and spent a year and a half developing their internal processes before they ever bid on the first contract. They had a clear vision, created their plan, and stayed focused, often working eighty to one hundred hours a week. It paid off when they were awarded the first contract they ever bid on.

Listening to the Right People

As soon as you begin pursuing your Plan B, you will automatically change how you act and what you think. And you'll talk differently about yourself, your dreams, your future, your goals, and your needs. As with most change, you will meet with resistance, often from those closest to you—your family, friends, or business associates—who may not encourage you. They may be jealous or feel threatened by the new you. Perhaps they are scared about losing the old you. If you are successful, they wonder, does that make them a failure? Some people will be convinced you are making a horrible mistake; others will feel vulnerable because it will change their world too. This is one reason your *why* must be bigger than your *but*.

Because others will try to "protect" you from yourself as you begin your journey, be sure to maintain your focus by asking yourself:

- Who am I listening to?
- Are they healthy, happy, and rich?
- Or are they unhealthy, fearful, and broke?

One test of "listening worthiness" comes from Joe Pici, the author of the Sell Naked book series and sales training.[4] Joe's theory is the *fresh fruit test*. Ask yourself these three questions:

- Are they more successful than I am?
- Are they presently doing their Plan B?
- Is their new fruit (their success) a result of their own efforts?

If so, then keep talking and keep listening! You want to be around people who will support and challenge you. Those who will call you on your stuff, challenge you on your actions and assumptions, and help when you are dragging your feet. They aren't going to let you play victim or spend time placing blame. They may not always be comfortable companions because they poke about, asking what you are doing and why.

Outside advisors or business coaches can help you here. Their entire focus is to help, question, and push you to keep moving.

Wrap Up

This chapter's purpose was to focus on you and you alone and to build on the work you have already done as you developed your *why*. Your mission was to learn what your Plan B journey may look like, the key traits of serial entrepreneurs, the five requirements of successful change, and how to listen to the right people.

The next chapter gives you an inside look at four business models for your Plan B. We'll compare and contrast them so you can more easily evaluate and decide which one(s) are the best matches for you, given all you've discovered about yourself recently. You will also learn how the wealthiest Americans have made their money.

The adventure continues in the next chapter…

Notes

1   Holly Wilder
    Sweet! Good Golly Miss Holly
    www.sweetbyholly.com

2   TTI Performance Systems, Ltd.
    www.ttiassessments.com

3   Luke & Associations, Inc.
    www.lukeassoc.com

4   Pici & Pici
    www.piciandpici.com

CHAPTER 4

There Are Many Paths to a Plan B

THE REALITIES OF LIFE are that you have to make a living and want to save enough for your retirement. The question is always, "How am I going to do it?" As we explored in chapter 1, the traditional job—your Plan A—may no longer be a viable answer.

In this chapter, you will learn how the wealthiest 1% makes its money. You were introduced to this topic in chapter 1, in which we explored the relative wealthiest of an average one hundred Americans at age sixty-five. This chapter will also cover what you need to pack for your upcoming Plan B journey, and we'll introduce the four Plan B options (each option has its own in-depth chapter later in the book).

Creating a Plan B allows you to leave behind bad bosses, discrimination, and unfair business practices. Plan B is all about you and the results you create. Refreshing and frightening, isn't it?

Here is one Plan B story from Shannon Wilburn, a stay-at-home mom:

> "As the mother of a one- and a three-year-old, I struggled with the high cost and short life of maternity and baby clothes. Maternity clothes are only needed for a few months, and the kids seem to grow out of their clothes in weeks. We certainly don't wear out our clothes.
>
> "To stretch my budget, I shopped consignment for these items. By the time my kids were toddlers, I had amassed a small inventory, so I decided to start a consignment business, mainly to put the good stuff I had found into the hands of other struggling moms. I could hear my own mother saying *waste not, want not.*
>
> "I started small by holding regular sales in my tiny living room. As word got around and more moms called me, I found a larger space for my sales events. I worked hard, and there seemed to be an endless supply of merchandise to re-sell, so it kept growing. I was eventually able to franchise my system and now it's a $20 million business."

Out of frustration, a simple business was born, nurtured, and grown. *Just Between Friends* is fourteen years old, with more than one hundred franchises hosting JBF Sales Events in twenty-two states.[1]

Shannon created and grew a multi-million-dollar business; imagine what you can do!

The traditional Plan A job gives you one-to-one income generation. You show up, you work, and you get paid. You are trading time for money. If you stop working, then the money stops too. And, as you know, this really isn't the best way to achieve early retirement or to create wealth.

The exercises in chapter 2 were designed to help you explore your bigger dreams so you could find your *why*. Your *why* is the key that opens the door to a Plan B. Perhaps you long to travel for fun or to spend more time on your hobbies. Some people want to leave an inheritance for their family. Each time I ask a close friend what he wants, he always says, "to be a philanthropist."

Whatever bigger dreams you have identified are the reasons you will be ready to move forward.

If you've realized your Plan A is not your long-term solution, then you need more options. So let's look at what you will need on your journey, and then introduce the core business models that will provide a framework for evaluating your ideas.

Start Packing for Your Journey

Here is what you need to pull together to help you decide what kind of Plan B you will create:

- **Your *why*.** You created this in chapter 2 as you evaluated your values and what you do and don't want in your life. Your *why* will give you the push you need to begin and keep going. As part of your hero's journey, this begins your departure.

> Going confidently into the future is like packing for a trail; you want to be sure to take everything you need, but not everything you own.
>
> It is a good feeling to know you have packed just the right stuff for your journey. The mistake most of us make is burdening ourselves with too much baggage.
>
> Ask yourself, "Am I packing the best of the past for the trip into the future?"
>
> —Bob New,
> AUTHOR,
> *LOOKING FOR THE GOOD STUFF...*
> A GUIDE TO ENJOYING AND APPRECIATING LIFE.[2]

- **Mindset to create your future.** This will also come from the work you have done when you created your *why* and the ideas you are already considering. You must be excited, focused, and anticipate your new future. Your intention for your Plan B will determine your focus. Remember that what you focus on will expand, so you want to always be looking at what you want to create and not obsessively focus on the mistakes you have made. (This is something I have to keep reminding myself.)

- **Right opportunity with the right timing.** You will need a growing customer base that is ready to repeatedly buy what you offer. In chapter 5, we will go into more detail about methods to evaluate your idea so you can avoid costly mistakes. In chapter 6, you will learn more about the core requirements of a successful business.

- **New skills.** Being a lifelong learner really comes in handy here. There is a lot to learn as you create your Plan B. If you like learning, your journey will be more fun and exciting.

- **Proven training.** There are many things to learn as you create and grow your business. Some of your Plan B path options, such as deciding to buy a franchise, will provide established training and procedures so all you have to do is learn them and follow the directions. Other options, such as starting a company, will require you to find other professionals who specialize in what you will need to learn. No matter which option you choose, plan to invest in training for yourself and your staff.

- **Right team.** There is no one I know who can do everything by themselves and, besides, you'll want some companions on your journey. The tricky part is to make sure you align yourself with people you can trust, who are dependable, and who can do what you can't. Family members are typically the easiest and most common place to start.

Four Ways to Create Your Plan B

Here are the four basic ways to create your Plan B. Pretty much any idea you have can fit into one of these four. The model's value is that you will learn about the advantages, risks, and varying levels of investment in time and money before you begin. By the time you finish chapter 10, you will know the good, the bad, and the ugly of each of the four Plan B options.

A common but valuable piece of advice when starting anything new: don't quit your day job. This is also good advice for you as you work on your Plan B. Once you put it in place, it may take time before you can write yourself your first paycheck. Your Plan B is really the process of building your own business over time; it is about investing time and effort now for a future payout. Be smart and don't quit your job to jump into your Plan B too soon. A good rule of thumb is to keep your current job until Plan B income equals your Plan A income for over a year.

Here's another way to look at it. Building your Plan B is like losing those pesky fifteen pounds that have piled on over the last few years. You are not going to lose all fifteen of them in one day of dieting. It will take time, focus, and new behaviors.

Remember that as you build your Plan B, making one hundred phone calls or passing out one hundred flyers in one day will not result in an additional one hundred customers. Those actions are just the beginning of what you will do to build a profitable Plan B business.

Overview of the Four Plan B Options

Plan B Options	Start your own business	Buy a business	Buy a franchise	Network marketing
Description of the option	You have an option to create a business	You purchase a business that already exists	You buy a business that expands by duplicating itself through selling franchises	You become a distributor, which means you sell other's products or services and recruit others to do the same
Level of investment of time and money	High investment of time and money	High investment of time and money	High investment of time; monetary investment will vary	Investment of time will vary; money investment is low
Estimated risk	High failure rate because most owners haven't read this book or understand the core business basics	Potentially lower failure rate because of established customers and processes	Potentially lower failure rate because of established products/ services and business processes	Failure rate varies: lower failure rate if sales happen and new distributors are recruited. Higher failure rate if sales skills are not mastered
Level of training already available	No training; you have to find it on your own	Training from current owners	Training is part of the purchase price with established processes	Training from those who recruited you, from the company, and professional sales trainers
Level of branding and marketing already available	You create your own branding and marketing	Current owner has already created and implemented branding and marketing	Potentially world-class branding and marketing	Potentially world-class branding and marketing

For a successful Plan B, you will have to be passionate about either your business or about making money. If you aren't passionate about one or the other, you will not likely be successful because it is the passion that will keep you going when things get rough.

What is the right Plan B for you? You've already started this process of discovery by doing the exercises in chapters 2 and 3. In chapter 2, you learned what key areas of your life you are satisfied with and where you want to improve. You identified what you don't and do want in your life. In chapter 3, you learned how your Plan B will be like a hero's journey, and the five requirements of successful change.

> "We don't make movies to make money; we make money to make more movies."
>
> —WALT DISNEY

But before we go any further, let's establish that money plays an important role in your Plan B. Most likely, it's a motivator for having and doing more of what you want. Remember the statistics from chapter 1 that showed the wealth status of one hundred Americans at age sixty-five? There was that one person in a hundred who was considered wealthy—who made over $250,000 a year.

Let's take a closer look at these people, called the Wealthy 1%, and see how they made their money. Here is what these top earners are doing:

The Wealthy 1%

- 10% are top professionals (doctors, dentists, and attorneys). It takes a lot of education and aptitude to achieve success in these professions, so it is unlikely this would be an option for most readers; you are probably not at a point in your life where you can go back to school for six to ten years.
- 10% of the CEOs in the United States are defined as wealthy. Their income comes from their base salaries, bonuses, and stock-option profits.
- 5% are super salespeople for big-ticket items like commercial jets and massive earth-moving equipment. They only need to sell a few each year to create significant income.

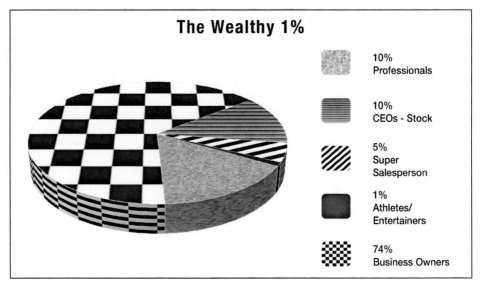

The New Interagency Report: Older Americans 2000:
Key Indicators of Well-Being (US Census)

- 1% are super athletes and entertainers. Oprah Winfrey and Derek Jeter are probably not realistic career models for most people.
- 74% of the wealthiest are business owners. This is the largest group, and there are a lot of reasons why you can join them.

Next is the short overview of the first of the Plan B options.

Starting Your Own Business

This book is the *real deal guide* to creating your business, which means you'll read some scary, unvarnished statistics here. As you take a look at them, keep in mind that most people who are part of these statistics have not done the work you already have and will complete by the time you finish this book. If they had, I feel confident the statistics would reflect higher levels of success.

Starting their own business is a dream for many people and it has created significant wealth for some. The risk is also high, because one-third of new businesses fail in the first year and 80% close their doors within the first three years (although various research studies show slightly different—but still similar—percentages). A lot of my research makes it pretty clear that most of these failed businesses were not well thought out to begin with. A good recipe for fried chicken does not make you the next Colonel Sanders, as my husband always says.

By the time you finish working through the tools and models in this book, you will have a clear understanding of your Plan B's strengths and weaknesses. Most of those business owners that failed did not take the time to gain the understanding you will have. Attend a new-member orientation at your local chamber of commerce and listen to the businesses introduce themselves—you'll see what I mean. It's clear which ones will not survive for such reasons as low demand for their offerings, a poor storefront location, low demand for repurchases, or the owner's inability to articulate the new venture's primary target market, for instance.

In addition to this book, there are endless resources for learning more about starting a business: from the government's Small Business Administration (SBA) to a wide variety of seminars, consultants, and, of course, other books. But expert advice is not the total solution. If your *why* is big enough, your determination is solid, your concept is viable, and your timing is good, then your skills—and a little luck—will make you successful.

To help ensure you are part of the group of successful business owners, chapter 7 has more in-depth information on starting a business. There, you will learn the two types of business start-ups, apply the Six Key Ingredients of successful businesses and be introduced to the Real Deal Checklist to help ensure your ideas are viable. You will learn the good and bad news about starting a business, as well as the advantages and disadvantages.

Next you will read an overview of the second of the Plan B options.

Buying an Existing Business

Buying a business can be easier than starting one. The products or services are in place, clients are established—as are sales—and you may have employees that come with the business too.

This book, your *real deal guide,* will show you how to determine if the business grew its client base due to the present owner's ability to form business relationships with the clients, or because of the quality of the products and services. If the business depends on the owner's relationships, make sure you have the skills and time to build your own relationships with those clients as quickly as possible. You don't want them to leave when the current owner leaves.

You may also want to consider working in the business (or shadow the owner) for a full business cycle before you buy. The cycle will vary and could be as short as a week, a calendar month, or even a full year, depending on what the company sells. For example, fast food restaurants' cycle could be as short as a week but a catering business would be closer to six months or a year because of the seasonal demands. Why would you want to work in the business so long? You want to know all of the costs (time, effort, and money) before you commit yourself to purchasing it. However 80%-90% of your work will be in analyzing the business financials.

There are tools and more information in chapter 8 to help you determine if you want to pursue this option. As always, you will learn the good and bad news about buying a business and the advantages and disadvantages. We will apply the Six Key Ingredients and the Real Deal Checklist, how to search for a business to buy, and the resources available to you. You'll learn which helpful, accessible documents to obtain and the analysis you should do on them.

The third of the four Plan B options is next.

Buying a Franchise

Franchises are attractive because they are a "business in a box," essentially, and may offer a higher success rate, more established branding, credible national advertising campaigns, and proven systems. The good news is that the learning curve is shorter because everything you do is dictated by the franchise system. The bad news is that everything you do is dictated by the franchise system, so if you like to tweak systems, this is probably not the option for you. The other potential downside is that most successful franchises are owner-run, so you, personally, may be on site and working most of the time.

Chapter 9 will provide more good and bad news about buying a franchise and additional advantages and disadvantages. In that chapter, we again apply such tools as the Six Key Ingredients of successful companies and the Real Deal Checklist. You will learn what controls and restrictions franchisors typically impose on you, the ins and outs of the four franchise models, how to conduct your own due diligence, and how to evaluate the experts that may be of help to you.

Then, finally, the fourth of the four Plan B options is next.

Network Marketing

Network marketing (also called *multi-level marketing, referral marketing, or direct sales*) is a distribution system of selling products and services through people who are independent distributors. Commissions are paid on the sales of products and/or services and recruiting more distributors.

Network marketing can be attractive because the branding, products, systems, and training are already in place. The ability to expand, and therefore to earn more, is considered unlimited because you are not typically confined to a building or geographic territory. You earn residual income as your customers continue to buy the products or services, similar to insurance agents who continue to get a commission on policies they have sold and are renewed. The investment is minimal compared with starting or buying a business or a franchise.

Network marketing can also be an excellent training ground for someone who wants to find out what it would be like to own their own business. Everything you need is in place; your job is to sell the offerings. If you go this route, you will need to learn such business basics as how to make sales, manage your cash flow, and manage time and priorities. In fact, if you are only familiar with working in a Plan A-type job and have not already mastered the business behaviors you will need for your

Plan B; this is the recommended place to start. If you can be successful here, you will have many of the critical skills needed for any of the other Plan B options.

Chapter 10 has more information on network marketing and how to choose the best companies, as well as the good and bad news and the advantages and disadvantages of network marketing. It also addresses the confusion some people have about the industry, and how to find a good company, then evaluate which person within the organization you want to work with. Of course, we also apply the Six Key Ingredients and the Real Deal Checklist, and we do this by looking closely at two anti-aging products.

Wrap Up

You now know the Wealthy 1% are business owners, and what you need to pack for your upcoming Plan B journey to your own wealth. You have a basic understanding of the four Plan B options and what you can expect to find in the chapters on each one of them.

The next chapter will build on your work from chapter 2 by helping you think through your Plan B idea. You'll explore where you will find the time and money to start your Plan B. Then you will determine your preferred work lifestyle by finding the type of work you like, what you want your average workday to be like, and where you will be working from. You will determine what mental and physical stamina is required, and the emotional toll your option will take. Finally, you will begin with the end in mind as you identify your exit strategy from the successful Plan B company you own.

Join me for the next part of your journey…

Notes

1 Shannon Wilburn
Just Between Friends
www.jbfsale.com

2 Bob New
Looking for the Good Stuff...a guide to enjoying
and appreciating life
AllStar Printing, Inc., May 2003, page 31
www.lookingforthegoodstuff.com

CHAPTER 5

Thinking It Through:

Avoiding the Pitfalls of Wrong (and Costly) Decisions

THIS BOOK IS PERSONAL. It is coming from my heart, not just my head, primarily because I made many, many mistakes as I searched for and tested Plan B ideas. When I left my Plan A job in the corporate world, I was an expert in my profession. I knew how to fix problems for my company. However, because I was burned out and eager for a change, I jumped into a Plan B without more thought than I would give to buying a new suit.

I eventually realized I simply did not have the right tools or structure to guide me on my journey to create a successful Plan B business. There were questions I did not know to ask myself or other people. As a result, I lost a lot of money, time, and sleep—but *you* don't have to! In this chapter, we'll present a useful and efficient structure for thinking through the critical factors in any Plan B. In chapter 2, you determined your *why;*

in this chapter, you will decide where some of the resources you need will come from, such as time and money. You will also identify your preferred work lifestyle, such as where you want to work from (i.e., a storefront, home office, or the road), what you want your workday to be like, the energy that will be required, and the emotional toll the work will bring with it. Lastly, you will begin thinking about your exit strategy.

As a result of the work you will do in this chapter, you will enjoy success faster and more easily, and have fewer unpleasant surprises.

Here is another story about mistakes I made and learned from. I am sharing it so you can avoid my pain and experience only the gain.

> I thought going into business with Gary meant I was on my path to the right start-up with the right product and the right business partner. We were both fans of Oprah Winfrey, Wayne Dyer, and Deepak Chopra, and our business's mission, we decided, was to help others. Specifically, to help charities increase their cash flow. Neither of us had started a business before, but we were smart people and willing to work hard. Everything was coming together, and it was so serendipitous that I just knew it was meant to be.

> I soon made several personal loans to Gary from my retirement account because he was working full-time to get the business going (I was working part-time on it). We made great progress and things looked very promising.

Just when Gary was ready to have an independent auditor verify the very complex website development work the developers said they had completed, we got a shock from their attorneys. It turned out we had not read the contract carefully enough or had it reviewed by an attorney of our own. So instead of giving us access with the independent auditor, they told us the final payment was due in full and, by the way, they owned the website content—not us. They owned all the work we had paid them to do!

For starters, this meant that if we decided at some later point to work with other web designers (hopefully because the company was growing and evolving, and thus had different needs), we would have to pay the new company to redesign an entirely new website. To start from scratch, because what we had—such as the programming code and the graphics—was not really ours to change and adapt, despite having paid for its creation and implementation. The website developers were holding us hostage, and we were running out of time and money. *My* money.

Because I, too, was focused on the start-up, my own consulting company was running out of clients and cash. The start-up business had looked like fun in the beginning, but I eventually realized my first love was consulting and executive coaching. So while I had departed on a new journey with the start-up and gone through the initiation, I heard my call to return and followed it.

It's been over four years since I returned to my business. Gary has since filed for bankruptcy. I personally lost more than $100,000 that will never be recovered. Other investors lost even more. I had thought I was pretty smart, but this was stupid, stupid, stupid.

Some of my lessons learned from this expensive and humbling experience are:

> "Do not cheap out on attorneys. You can use tape to hem your skirt, but do not cheap out on an attorney."
>
> —WENDY LIPTON-DIBNER, MA, PRESIDENT, PROFESSIONAL IMPACT, INC., AND AUTHOR[1]

- Do not equate sharing similar interests and heroes with having successfully found a business partner. Instead, look first for skills, experience, and expertise.
- If your partner can't pay his or her own bills, move on. Few things will change as the demands of the new venture increase. Partners need to bring their own money to the table because they will have to build the business without paying themselves a salary until the business consistently makes a profit.
- It is imperative to find and use legal and financial experts with savvy in your Plan B's industry. Have the experts review everything before you sign anything.

Fortunately, I learn quickly and won't make these same mistakes again. And maybe you've learned enough from my wretched experience that you can avoid anything similar.

If I had been able to read this *real deal guide,* I'm confident that the outcome of that situation would have been very different. I would have known the right questions to ask, had sufficient information on how to analyze a business idea, and gotten to my *no* a lot faster. The tools would have helped to cool my enthusiasm and to open my eyes to reality, and I would not have lost the money and time I did.

By using what you learn in this book, you won't make the same mistakes I did. You will more quickly realize when an idea or opportunity has too much uncertainty or risk associated with it. You will gain perspective and hopefully have the resolve to walk away from seductive deals that don't measure up under cold, hard scrutiny. The key is *thinking* through your plan.

A Structure for Thinking Through Your Plan B

No matter which Plan B option you pursue, you'll need a structure such as that described below. By identifying early in your process what is possible, you will move forward with a clear vision of what will work best for you.

This topic actually has two sections—two structured methods—for you to work with. The first section is designed to help you decide where you'll find the time and money for your Plan B. For some people, this is the scary part, because this is where they will either step up and take control of their future—or not. That is the reason you created your powerful *why* in chapter 2. The second section guides you through a structured process to find your preferred work lifestyle. But let's start with time and money.

Critical Resources for All Businesses

Two resources are critical to all businesses:

- **Time:** Where will you find the time to start your Plan B?
- **Money:** How much money will you need to invest? Where will it come from?

Time

Where will you find the time to create your Plan B? In business, there is no "sometime"—there is only full time and part-time and overtime (i.e., evenings and weekends). If you are not currently working, then you could and probably should devote your full attention to your Plan B. If you still need to collect a paycheck to pay the bills, then start working on your Plan B on a part-time basis and then, as you build the business, it can become your full-time focus.

The point is that you must block out and schedule the time. It cannot be sometime, because sometime is whenever you get around to it, which likely means you won't do it consistently and, like an ill-tended garden, it won't be very fruitful.

To get started, look at how you spend your time now. Analyze your calendar or day-planner to see where you have time that is open, or how you could change what you are currently doing to make room for this new project.

A fifty-something man I interviewed said he realized he was wasting at least three hours a day by spending too much time on Facebook and watching mindless television shows. He said, "Once I realized that, I suddenly had fifteen to twenty hours each week to work on my Plan B!"

One business consultant I have worked with has written thirteen books so far and is cranking out another one. He blocks out his time so he can write from 7:00 a.m. to 9:00 a.m. three days a week. He also writes on

> "For every hour you spend planning, you will save three hours in execution."
>
> This is an often-quoted statistic in time- and project-management circles. But if you don't have the skills or tools to do a good job planning, then you will be like a hamster on its wheel—going nowhere fast and quickly using up your resources.
>
> —KATHLEEN RICH-NEW, BUSINESS CONSULTANT, SPEAKER, EXECUTIVE COACH, CLARITY WORKS CONSULTING; AUTHOR, PLAN B

Saturday or Sunday if he was not able to stick to his regular weekday schedule. Needless to say, he sells a lot of books.

Take a few minutes to think about how you will find time in your own life to work on your Plan B. Use the blanks below to identify where you will find the time and how much you will have.

The number of hours and the time of day I will commit to working on my Plan B:

Monday:
Number of hours_____ Time of day_____

Tuesday:
Number of hours_____ Time of day_____

Wednesday:
Number of hours_____ Time of day_____

Thursday:
Number of hours_____ Time of day_____

Friday:
Number of hours_____ Time of day_____

Saturday:
Number of hours_____ Time of day_____

Sunday:
Number of hours_____ Time of day_____

To find more time, I'll identify what I will:
start doing: _____
stop doing: _____

Some of your answers will come from the results of your Life Values Model in chapter 2, which should give you ideas on where more time can come from. For example, if you are over-the-top satisfied with your Play & Fun wedge or the Social aspect of your life, perhaps some of that time and energy can be shifted to your Plan B option.

Money

Your Plan B will obviously require money. How much available money do you have to invest in it? How soon will your Plan B make a profit? Because I am assuming you are creating a Plan B to make money—versus having a hobby or creating a social life—this is one of your critical planning areas. As I've mentioned before, you would also be well served to work with financial experts experienced in the type of Plan B option you are considering.

> Banks aren't going to lend you money for a start-up business. You will need to get it from the famous three Fs: family, friends, and fools.
>
> —POPULAR ADAGE

Your amount of available money and resources will determine which businesses you can afford. The type of business you choose, as well as the skills you bring, will determine how much income and the level of wealth you can create.

There is more specific information on how much money you will likely need for three of the four Plan B options—buying a business, buying a franchise, and network marketing—in each respective chapter. (If you are considering starting a company, the amount of money you need can vary greatly. One reality to consider is that it may take several years before you make a profit. Meanwhile, you will need to have enough money to pay your personal bills as well those of your business.) For each Plan B option, you will determine your break-even point so you can calculate how long it will take to start making money. Again, experts can help you with this.

To get started, grab a pencil and a piece of paper (or sit down at your computer), and use this great tool to identify potential sources of investment money for your Plan B:

1. Amount of personal savings that is available
2. Extra money currently available at the end of each month (multiplied by 12 months)
3. Family members willing to invest. What are the terms (interest, partial ownership, or…)?
4. Friends willing to invest. What are the terms (interest, partial ownership, or…)?
5. Other individuals who are interested in nvestment opportunities. What are the terms?
6. Assets you could sell (collections, investments, houses, cars, art, etc.)

Add up the money you have identified in items one through six, and you'll know how much you have available for an initial investment.

Your total may be just a few hundred dollars, or tens of thousands, or maybe even over a million dollars. The amount of money you have available will directly impact the Plan B options available to you. The chapters on the four Plan B options will provide additional insight and information on this topic.

For now, here are some preliminary points to ponder…

Starting a business can be inexpensive if you work from a home office and already have the office equipment you need. There are costs associated with obtaining a business license and insurance coverage, and you may also need to purchase inventory. If you are already in a niche industry or a community that is interested in doing business with you, you may be able to make quick and easy sales based on your relationships. So while you could find it easy to get started, you still need to be able to pay your expenses as you grow your company large enough to make a profit.

Buying a business will typically require a 30%–40% down payment. Often the owner/seller will hold the remainder of the loan with agreed-upon payment terms. Or you may be able to go to a lending institution. Some provide a loan based on your credit score, the value of the business' accounts receivable, and/or any collateral you have—a home or other investments, such as stocks and bonds. One of the experts in chapter 8 tells us purchasing existing businesses with more than $100,000 in annual sales have a higher level of continuing success.

The purchase price to *buy a franchise* can range from $30,000 to over $2 million, but one expert in chapter 9 said it's hard to buy a good one for less than $50,000. The franchisor's fee buys you the franchisor's trade name and systems; you will also need to factor in such secondary investment requirements as facilities, inventory, and ongoing fees charged by the franchisor.

Network marketing investments can technically be just a few dollars, but you will likely need some inventory, which ranges from a few hundred to a couple of thousand dollars. Even so, this is the least expensive Plan B. It is sometimes referred to as the *poor person's franchise.*

Because the amount of money you have to invest will directly impact your choice of a Plan B, use the work you did in chapter 2 to help match you to the one(s) that will work the best for you. The work lifestyle section below will also help.

Finding Your Work Lifestyle

In this section you will identify the *work lifestyle* you want. Work lifestyle is what your average workday will be, day after day, in the Plan B you create. Your answers will indicate which of the Plan B options are good a match and which ones aren't. As we have already recommended, there's merit in deciding which ones are not good matches because then you won't waste time exploring them.

Specifically, the work lifestyle exercise guides you to determine the:

1. *Type of work* you will do
2. *Type of people* you will interact with
3. *Location* of where you will work
4. *Energy,* or the mental and physical stamina needed to do the work
5. *Emotional toll,* as the work either excites you or drains you
6. *Exit strategy,* which includes how long you plan to work in the business, as well as how you will end your involvement in it

These six areas will define much of your preferred work lifestyle. Let's get started!

1. Type of Work

We all have a preference for the type of work we do, which typically comes from what we find easy and what we are good at. There is no one type of work that is better than the other. The only thing that matters is what works best for you.

For each pair below, circle or highlight whichever one most appeals to you. Go as fast as you can and don't dwell on what it should be. Just go with your first thought.

- Variety *vs.* routine work
- Problem solver *vs.* implementer doing the work
- Requires a lot of thinking *vs.* physically demanding
- Creative work *vs.* use what has worked before
- People (friends, family, fun) *vs.* task (details, dollars, deadlines)
- Other (what else appeals to you about the type of work you like to do?)

You will typically see a pattern to your answers. Some people I have worked with are exiting a career that required them to be a creative problem solver. Now they just want to fix problems and help others. There is no right or wrong answer because it is about you. And only you.

2. Type of People

All of the Plan B options include interacting with people—customers, suppliers, or employees, for example. Some business owners feel they need to be around other people, while other business owners and professionals simply want to be left alone to work solo. What is the best match for you?

As in the previous section, circle or highlight whichever one most appeals to you.

- Lots of people around *vs.* work alone
- People who make quick decisions *vs.* slow decisions
- People who don't care about details *vs.* love details
- People who challenge my ideas *vs.* no challenges
- People who appreciate me *vs.* doesn't matter
- People who are well educated and brainy *vs.* doesn't matter
- Other (what else appeals to you about the people you like to work with?)

Your answers will piece together the people you want to work with and those you don't. There will be no absolutes, of course, but this certainly indicates your preferences. As a result, you can more easily determine the best Plan B for you.

3. Location of Your Work

Where will your Plan B require you to physically be? Today's technology allows a lot more flexibility than we have had in the past. Some Plan B options, such as a storefront, require working from the same location; others allow you to work from almost anywhere.

Try this short exercise to get clear on what type of work location would be best for you. Rate each item on a 1-to-5 scale, with 1 = strongly disagree, 2 = disagree, 3 = neutral/doesn't matter, 4 = agree, and 5 = strongly agree.

_____ I never want to leave my house/office/
computer

_____ My customers will come to me in my
office or store

_____ I want to earn the Road Warrior Award
for the most frequent-flyer miles on at
least three airlines

_____ My theme song should be "On the Road
Again," because I love to drive to
customers' locations

_____ Other (what else appeals to you about
your work location?)

Your answers will help you identify the Plan B that most closely aligns with the physical location and conditions that best suit you. If you have very strong feelings about being able to work from anywhere, then you'll immediately reject such options as buying a brick-and-mortar business and some types of franchises.

4. Energy Required, i.e., Your Physical and Mental Stamina

This section encourages you to consider an area of life that people don't usually think about other than to say that something does not excite them. For example, the physical stamina required to install landscaping in the middle of a hot, steamy Florida summer takes an entirely different level of energy than does sitting at a desk in an air-conditioned building and working on a computer all day. While the stamina required to run your business may not matter too much in the beginning, you will be working in your Plan B business for at least three years and could be at it for ten years or more.

You should also consider travel requirements and time zones. For example, you may have clients on the opposite coast or in Europe or Asia. Talking with them may mean you are on the phone at 11:00 p.m. or even 3:00 a.m. If you need to meet with them personally, keep in mind you'll spend time in airports, changing time zones, and feeling jet-lagged. Travel demands can interfere with your sleep schedule and time with your family.

Mental exhaustion can also impact your stamina, especially if your work requires long hours of intense concentration with little moving around.

Mark an X where you are most comfortable with the *physical* demands of the work you prefer:

Sit down   Fairly active   Move
                                         around

|_____|_____|_____|_____|

For example, working in a retail store may require you to stand on your feet all day. Other work may require you to be in front of a computer hour after hour. What is your preferred level of physical activity?

Now, let's look at the mental demands of your Plan B career.

Mark an X where you are most comfortable with the *mental* demands of the work you prefer:

Easy and   Good for two   Able to stay
mindless   to three hours   concentrated
work   of concentration   and focused
effort   all day   all day

|_____|_____|_____|_____|

All Plan B options have mental demands, but some will require a very specific way of doing business, and others you will have to figure out on your own. Keep this in mind as you consider the various options.

5. Emotional Toll

This is another area few people think or talk about. You need to determine if, at the end of each day, you will be emotionally exhausted or excited and enthusiastic about your work. No job will ever provide excitement each day without any issues or challenges, of course. It's more a question of whether you will start each day with dread and loathing or with anticipation and joy.

It is important to remember you will build your Plan B business for several years, so what you do every day does make a difference in your life.

Choose the option that plays to your strengths and you will find life is easier:

Everything	A little drama	Nothing is
should be	is okay	better than
easy, with		a crisis
no drama		

|_____|_____|_____|_____|

6. Exit Strategy

Finally, before you enter into any Plan B agreement, you need to determine your exit strategy. You may not know yet what that strategy will look like, so you may need more time to decide. And that's okay.

Meanwhile, here are some more points to ponder: Your strategy may be triggered by a certain age or a date. Or perhaps you want to build a big enough or valuable enough business that you can sell it in five years. There may be intellectual property that creates a passive income stream, such as royalties paid to you for every item sold. Maybe you want to build a business that your children will take over and run for you. Or it could be that you will just close the doors when you have reached your goal.

By proactively thinking this through now, you will dramatically increase the likelihood that you will achieve it. This decision will also help determine the direction of your company. For example, one international business owner told me his exit strategy for his pilot-training school was to either be acquired or to become a publicly traded company by offering shares of stock through an IPO (Initial Public Offering).

Selling your carefully nurtured creation can be traumatic. Consider these two retailers (their names have been changed) from one small Midwestern town:

> George Browning, a high-end men's clothing store owner, told me he had always planned to sell the business when he turned sixty-three. Ensuring the store's reputation remained strong was important to him, because he had seen what had happened to Griffin's Department Store, just across from him on Main Street.

> Joe Griffin, another successful local retailer, had sold his business—lock, stock, and barrel—including the name. The well-respected store went downhill rapidly under the new owners. Now, Griffin has a hard time enjoying his retirement because he's constantly embarrassed by the shoddy merchandise and the sleazy sales tactics of the store that still bears his name.

> Browning was not about to let that happen to him, so he carefully interviewed interested buyers. No one fit his criteria or matched his work ethic, so when the time came, he reluctantly took down his name from the building facade, sold the inventory and the fixtures, locked the door, and walked away.

Below are the most common exit strategies. I suggest you choose the two most compatible with your goals and ideals, and then explore them in more detail.

- Sell the business by a specific calendar date
- Sell the business when you reach a specific age

"Begin with the end in mind."

—STEPHEN R. COVEY, AUTHOR, *THE 7 HABITS OF HIGHLY EFFECTIVE PEOPLE*[2]

- Build the company so it can be acquired by a larger company, and you either join the new company or exit completely
- Take the company public by selling shares of stock through an IPO
- Close the business

You may not be ready just yet to decide on an exit plan, but it is something you will eventually decide. Sooner is better than later.

Wrap Up

Well done! You now have a solid grounding in what you can and will bring to your Plan B, and what will be the best match and the most interesting. Because you are thinking through your business idea well in advance of implementing it, you will launch your business from a much stronger position. You have done more work and know more about yourself than most people do, so you are claiming your powers to move forward.

In the next chapter, we shift away from focusing on you and instead start concentrating on businesses. You will learn the Six Key Ingredients of successful businesses and then determine how many of them to apply to each of your business ideas. Of course, we will provide you with examples of the ingredients so you can easily see how they work in real-life situations.

Your journey's next step is in the very next chapter...

Notes

1   Wendy Lipton-Dibner, MA
    President, Professional Impact, Inc.
    Founder of Move People To Action™
    Author of:
    —*Shatter Your Speed Limits™ - Fast-Track Your Success and Get What You Truly Want in Business and in Life*
    —*M.A.D. (Motivate-Align-Differentiate) Leadership for Healthcare - Proven Strategies to Get People To Do What You Want Them To Do*
    www.pro-impact.com

2   Stephen R. Covey
    Author of:
    The 7 Habits of Highly Effective People, Powerful Lessons in Personal Change
    (New York: Simon and Schuster, 1989), 95.

CHAPTER 6

Six Key Ingredients of the Most Successful Businesses

AS ANY GOOD CHEF KNOWS, certain key ingredients are necessary if the dish is to turn out well. Without those essentials, it may be edible but not remarkable. The same is true of your Plan B business; you may survive but not become wildly successful.

Any profitable business needs Six Key Ingredients[1]:

1. Favorable market trends
2. Consumable products or ongoing services
3. Perfect timing
4. Strong compensation or attractive margins
5. Powerful partnerships
6. Unique products or exclusive technology

Few will be able to create a Plan B that has all of the Six Key Ingredients, but you certainly want to try for as many as possible. Here's an example of how the ingredients can blend together well:

About to have their first child, Jason and Kim Graham-Nye faced the facts: when you have a baby, you need diapers. But cloth diapers take a lot of water to wash. Disposable diapers clog our world's landfills and can take five hundred years to break down. A typical baby averages sixty diapers a week until the child is toilet trained—an average of five thousand diapers per baby. The environmentally concerned Jason and Kim went searching for an eco-friendly alternative to traditional diaper choices.

They found a company in Tasmania with a hybrid option—a reusable, cloth outer garment with a disposable, biodegradable absorbent pad. The combo diapers were just what the couple was looking for: no plastic, no elemental chlorine, no latex, and no dyes or perfumes. The pads are flushed down the toilet, put in the trash, or added to the home compost heap (where they break down in 50–150 days).

Jason and Kim saw a way to solve their personal concerns and also a business opportunity that fit their desire for a greener world. They negotiated the rights to the concept and created gDiapers. (The *g* stands for many things—genuine, global, green, grateful, etc.) The Graham-Nyes raised several million dollars and launched their business in the United States. The trendy, biodegradable gDiaper is now available online and in stores in the United States, Canada, the United Kingdom, and France.

The gDiapers product appears to have many of the Six Key Ingredients for a successful business and, so far, so good. They've hit the ground running. It will be interesting to follow their success during the next three to five years.[2]

Let's take a closer look at each of the Six Key Ingredients and apply them to gDiapers and to several other examples of products and services.

1. Favorable Market Trends

First, identify growing market trends and then determine how you can grow with them. This is one way to create a highly successful business. You want your market to be growing, or at least stable, but not shrinking.

What product and services will be in demand that are either not yet available or are not satisfying the markets' demands? For example, our population's increased obesity has led to more health issues and thus rising sales of such medical products as oversized wheelchairs, hospital beds, and furniture.

The green movement of being more environmentally and energy conscious has led to impressive innovation in a large variety of areas. One example is the plastic water bottle—the bane of landfills and the oceans. Some companies are replacing the traditional water bottle with a corn-based, plastic-like product that is biodegradable. With energy

> Starting on January 1, 2011, approximately 10,000 baby boomers per day will turn sixty-five, a pattern set for the next nineteen years.
>
> —PEW RESEARCH CENTER HTTP://PEWRE-SEARCH.ORG/ PUBS/1834/ BABY-BOOMERS-OLD-AGE-DOWNBEAT-PESSIMISM

costs high, the sale of Snuggies (a soft, warm blanket with sleeves) remains strong during the cold winter months.

gDiapers will ride the green movement market trend by appealing to environmentally concerned buyers with babies. It's likely that at some point, gDiapers will be proven more cost effective than other disposable diapers. The Graham-Nyes could also decide to apply the same diaper-hybrid technology to the fast-growing, adult-incontinence market.

Green products are gaining avid fans, often with significant help from legislative intervention. A great example is the energy-efficient compact fluorescent lightbulb, which emits the same light as classic incandescent bulbs but uses 75%–80% less electricity. Due to federal legislation, they are the only lightbulb available in the United States, starting in 2012. When that legislation was passed, China was the only country that manufactured the required bulbs, but American competitors are starting to produce the same thing.

2. Consumable Products or Ongoing Services

The cost of acquiring new customers is three to five times the cost of retaining your established ones.

—COMMONLY CITED STATISTIC

Frequent buyers, loyal customers, and what's referred to as "up-sells" (selling higher priced offerings to the same customers) are key to your success. If your typical customers only buy from you once, then you will have to keep finding new customers, which takes time and is expensive. Gillette, for instance, practically gives away its razors so consumers will keep buying Gillette razor blades.

Professional speakers usually offer products at a speaking engagement or seminar that attendees can purchase. The usual rule of thumb is to give something away for free—like a teleseminar or special report—and also offer something for less than $100, such as a training manual or a personal coaching session. Other products or services are available too, and their prices can climb to $25,000, for example, for a full day of consulting with a client on specific issues. Once people like and want more of what the speaker has to say and sell, they become clients who will buy additional products and services and will tell others about them.

Starbucks has certainly done a great job of creating loyal customers for their products, and the company makes the purchase transaction easy by providing Starbucks-branded, pre-purchased credit cards. McDonald's sales have remained strong during every recession; there's a lot to be learned there. And if gDiapers aligns with your environmental concerns and you need sixty diapers per week until your child's potty training is complete, you'll likely check out this innovative product.

3. Perfect Timing

No matter how bad (or good, for that matter) the economy may be, some businesses will be outrageously profitable while others struggle. There are no easy answers to when is a good time to start your Plan B plan, but there are a few tried-and-true theories to use as a starting point.

The *liquor and lipstick syndrome,* for instance, is a counter-cyclical profit pattern reminding us that, even in bad times, people spend money on what helps them feel better. To clarify, the term *counter-cyclical* in these examples means that when the economy goes down, some businesses will have an increase in sales. For example, if consumers replace their high-end cosmetic purchases with drugstore products, the drugstores' profits increase while the expensive cosmetic counters' coffers grow empty. Likewise, expensive liquor or wine may be replaced by inexpensive brands. Industry-wide, however, cosmetics and alcohol sales have historically remained strong in down economies, thus giving rise to the term *liquor and lipstick syndrome.* Consignment stores and thrift shops see increased sales when unemployment is high. Grocery store brands also see increased sales in a down economy.

Not every aspect of timing has to do with the economy. The introduction and growing sales of gDiapers is well timed with the increasing global concerns about the number of new landfills and the decreasing supply of water.

4. Strong Compensation or Attractive Margins

"Show me the money" is the quote everybody remembers from the movie, *Jerry Maguire,* about a sports agent trying to sign a professional football player as his client. Like that football player, you will want to be shown the money so you can see what you'll take home from your labors. In most traditional jobs, there is a direct connection between the hours you work and a predictable paycheck. You are trading time for money. In a commissioned sales job, it is all about how many sales you close. Your Plan B career can offer you a different option but you will need to determine just how profitable it can and will be.

For example, if you decide to open a brick-and-mortar location or even a virtual store, it will take time to attract clients who want and need your services on a regular basis. If you buy a company, you should be given profit projections you can actually use. If you sell a third party's products or services, you want to understand how much you will earn when you make a sale. gDiapers, our primary example in this chapter, is a private company, so specific financial information is not available. In a media interview, however, when gDiapers owner Kim was asked about being named by *Fortune* as one of the top ten female entrepreneurs, she said the company is profitable. We're not surprised!

Understanding how much income you'll earn is a critical requirement because, obviously, you want your Plan B to make money. Understanding *how* you will do it is one of the Six Key Ingredients to your success.

5. Powerful Partnerships

You can't and don't want to go it alone. If you have never successfully started your own business, get partners who have. Partners who have been to the peak of the mountain can show you the right trails, handholds, and rest spots. The right partners can help keep you from making a bad decision or at least warn you before you step off the proven path. They

> The entertaining Pet Rocks product earned $15 million in six months for Gary Dahl in 1975. It had attractive margins associated with a $3.95 retail price for, basically, a rock.
>
> -www.pesdo.com/
>
> The company rode their huge success by having just a few ingredients.
>
> But if he had added pet houses, hats, or sunglasses his profits would have increased dramatically.
>
> —KATHLEEN RICH-NEW,
>
> BUSINESS CONSULTANT, SPEAKER, EXECUTIVE COACH, CLARITY WORKS CONSULTING; AUTHOR, PLAN B

will see the warning signs that you would likely see only after you start sliding down the mountain.

Basically, business partnerships typically form in two ways: people who work directly with or for you, and business experts who offer their products and services to help you grow your business.

When starting a Plan B, you will naturally create partnerships with people who work with you in the business. Some partnerships are formed through thoughtful research and evaluation of the expectations, expertise, and experience each person brings. Others are formed more casually when acquaintances, friends, or family members come together.

Keep in mind that you can't build a successful business with pessimistic freeloaders; they will pull you and the business down. Instead, you need people who can and will pitch in and help when things aren't going exactly as planned. People with creativity and a great sense of humor are a bonus in any partnership. A rule of thumb for business and friends: it is better to go into business with skilled partners and become friends, than to be friends who go into business together and become enemies.

This is *your* Plan B; you are in charge. You will have to decide who you will allow to join you in developing your Plan B business. This is not the time to be a nice guy or gal by helping others out and allowing them to join you. If they don't add the specific value you need, they aren't allowed in. Period.

Here is a real-life example of what can go wrong, even when partners have the best of intentions:

> It is better to go into business with skilled partners and become friends, than to be friends who go into business together and become enemies.
>
> —ANONYMOUS

When fifty-five-year-old Sam realized his Plan A job would not meet his future needs, he looked around for other options. Charlie, a friend from church, introduced him to an investment opportunity to become a silent partner in a hurricane-panel business. As a silent partner, Sam would put up the money and the others would do the work.

The hurricane panel products were new to the hurricane panel industry. The large sheets of lightweight plastic were ideal to replace the heavy plywood panels typically used to board over windows and patio doors in anticipation of a hurricane. Most hurricane damage occurs when flying debris or extremely strong winds break windows, and these particular panels had proven to effectively prevent projectile and wind damage. The plastic panels were also lighter, easier to mount, and did not warp or splinter like plywood does. And the panels let in natural light, a definite improvement over the plywood boards that make homes' interiors dark and depressing when the power goes out, as usually happens in hurricanes. Almost every homeowner or storefront owner who saw the panels wanted them, so the demand was there.

The plan showed a three-year payback, followed by a share of the ongoing profits. Allen, who was in charge of running the business, was a well-connected, professional construction contractor.

What Sam did not know or anticipate was Allen's poor heart health. While unloading the first shipment of hurricane panels, Allen suffered a heart attack and died. To protect his investment, Sam reluctantly found himself at the top of a ladder, installing hurricane panels on two-story houses.

The building codes soon caught up with the new technology, and the panels were included in more restrictive local ordinances. Sam could no longer install them without Allen's contractor's license. As a result, Sam had to shut down the business and sell off the inventory and equipment to try to recover some of his investment. When I last talked to Sam, he still had about twenty of the original two thousand panels on hand.

This is an example of a partnership between two people who thought they had found a Plan B that worked for both of them. Several of the Six Key Ingredients were present: market trends were in Sam's favor because lighter hurricane panels reduced the number of back injuries from hefting heavy plywood. That alone made them attractive for homeowners. The panels were not consumable, but customers were referring their neighbors and friends to Sam. The timing could be labeled neutral to slightly negative, because hurricane season in the Atlantic begins June 1 and ends November 30, and buyers are only interested in the product when hurricanes are on the radar. The margins were profitable because the product was so new and appealing. But the partnership became a problem because of Allen's bad heart. And then there was the unanticipated installation restriction from new local ordinances.

While this business start-up had a few of the Six Key Ingredients, it didn't have enough of them. If Sam had known what to look for when he originally evaluated the opportunity, he may very well have reached a different decision about becoming a silent partner, or he would have at least looked into insurance on his partner.

Remember: anyone joining you—or with whom you're considering joining—must earn that right through past successes, current skills, and/or critical knowledge.

The second type of partnership is with business experts who offer products and services you will purchase, such as bankers and attorneys; experts in marketing, sales, and human resources; and Realtors and insurance agents. For example, bankers can help you find sources of funding, skilled accountants, and flexible lines of credit. Attorneys ensure any business contracts have terms that are favorable to you, and that you are making smart business decisions. Marketing and sales experts help you attract the most profitable type of customers and then to close those sales. Experts in human resources can help you find employees that are a good match for you personally and for the demands of the business. Realtors assist you with finding offices or storefronts that meet your requirements. Insurance agents provide you with the coverage you want and need.

Be sure to partner with experts who specialize in the type of Plan B business you are creating. For example, if you want to start a company, seek experts who specialize in business start-ups. If you are buying a franchise, find franchise experts. Be sure to find out how many clients and businesses they have worked with. Then talk with their clients on what it is like to work with them. You

> "Be not afraid of growing slowly; be afraid only of standing still."
>
> —CHINESE PROVERB

will also want to ask how the expert helped them grow their businesses.

We can safely assume gDiapers has powerful partnerships, because their products are in select retailers, such as Whole Foods and Babies"R"Us, and in four countries.

6. Unique Products or Exclusive Technology

This may be the most difficult of the Six Key Ingredients for the average person to achieve because it typically involves research and development costs that are beyond the reach of most of us. But keep reading, because this section can still give you some ideas. And that is what this book is about—helping you with ideas and options.

Having *unique products* means customers have to come to you and your organization because what you offer is not available anywhere else. *Exclusive technology* means you have developed and patent-protected your invention. Apple Computer is an example of introducing both unique products and exclusive technology. The iTunes store allows iPod owners, and those with other MP3-players, to legally download only the songs they want. iTunes became an instant hit and still dominates the market. Then the iPhone became a must-have for many users, in part because it offers more than 425,000 unique, downloadable applications for a variety of fun and business uses. Now the iPad is showing up in board rooms as the preferred way to take notes and instantly access the internet.

With our society's increased focus on personal appearance, the first companies to market with products that offer real results can often dominate early on. For example, teeth whitening was, at first, only available in dentists' office. Now you can buy similar products at grocers or drugstores, or have it done at a kiosk in the mall. Tanning beds are another popular example of the emphasis on personal appearance, despite the serious concerns about the long-term health risks. Many professional sports teams want their cheerleaders to look tan but were hesitant to insist the young women go tanning. Today, the spray-on tanning products used by cheerleaders are offered in a take-home version or through other beauty-service providers such as hair salons and fitness centers.

In these examples, adding a new twist on an existing popular product worked for companies that arrived late to the market. When you create your own Plan B, look at current best-selling products and services and determine if you can offer them in a unique way.

Exclusive technology can also be disruptive technology. Look at what happened to Kodak and the photographic film industry. Digital cameras have almost made film unnecessary and Kodak filed for bankruptcy. The Walkman transformed the music recording industry by allowing listeners to enjoy their favorite music and radio shows on the go. Vinyl records and cassette tapes have since been bumped off the hill by CDs, digital downloads, and MP3 players.

Each of these examples hopefully gives you some ideas. Look closely at what helped and what hurt these companies' sales. Do the same for your own business: Determine what products and services are in the works that might disrupt your business. There is no market for buggy whips, no matter how good they might be.

gDiapers's unique products have components that are protected by patents, and others that are made using "secret sauces" developed by the company. They're counting on significant competition at some point, so they have also created a strong brand in their niche as an additional line of defense.

Universal Truths for Business Success

There are three often-repeated truths about business that I have heard again and again. They make sense to me and will to you too.

1. *Nothing happens until someone sells some thing.* You can create the world's best mousetrap but if you can't sell it, then it doesn't matter. To make money in your Plan B, you must be able to sell your product and/or services. If you have only had non-sales jobs in the past, then this is a skill you can and must learn.
2. *You will have to become someone bigger and better.* If you want to play at a higher and more successful level, then there will be more to learn. This is the fun part.
3. *Nothing is an overnight success.* The media wants us to believe that success comes magically and from being at the right place at the right time. Spanx founder Sara Blakely is the world's youngest self-made female billionaire. She used $5,000 from savings and

worked out of the back of her apartment, and she did a whole lot of internet research, patent-writing, cold-calling, and less-than-shy demonstrations for buyers. She created the product and the company while selling fax machines door to door.

Wrap Up

You now know the Six Key Ingredients that the most successful businesses all have. Some highly successful businesses prove that it's okay to have only a few of the ingredients, however, the more you do have, the stronger your business will be.

The following chapters provide detailed information on the four paths to creating a Plan B: start a business, buy a business, buy a franchise, and network marketing. You will also learn the good, the bad, and the ugly aspects about each path because, after all, this is your *real deal guide.*

Your hero's journey really picks up speed in the next chapter. I recommend you read all four chapters unless you've already ruled out a particular path. (Even then, each chapter contains useful information that applies to other Plan B paths, so at least skimming the chapters you're currently ruling out is a good idea.)

Chapter 7 shows what is involved in starting your own business, and we'll take a closer look at the two types of start-ups. So that you get the *real deal* about starting a business, we'll cover the advantages and disadvantages of taking this path to your Plan B. You will also be introduced to the Real Deal Checklist and learn how to use it as we apply it to a consulting-practice idea.

Are you ready to continue your journey? It's time to paddle out into the ocean on your surfboard so you can catch the next big wave...

Notes

1   Adapted from *System 7 – Five-Point Presentation,* One Team Global, January 2010, Melbourne Beach, FL

2   gDiapers
www.gdiapers.com

CHAPTER 7

The Real Deal about Starting Your Own Business

STARTING A BUSINESS means you decide what products and/or services you want to offer that others are willing to buy. You must create something brand new or duplicate what someone else is already doing. You are responsible for creating what you will need to run a business; the offerings, the marketing and sales, and the operations. You are responsible for non-revenue-producing activities such as accounting, facilities management, and complying with various government regulations. You also either personally finance the start-up or find the money elsewhere, and you need to pay both your business and personal bills until you start making a profit.

This is the first of four chapters that will go in depth on the proven ways to create a Plan B.

By applying what you have already learned about yourself from the exercises in chapters 2 and 5, you can narrow your choices to the ones that best match you. In chapter 6, you learned to evaluate a business' potential by using the Six Key Ingredients as a first-pass filter. If the potential business registers as a strong contender, then you will want to continue your analysis with the Real Deal Checklist introduced in this chapter.

Starting your own business can be a satisfying and rewarding experience. It can create wealth and fund your retirement when you sell it. Or you can use it to create a legacy to pass down to other members of your family. You could become an icon in your community as you grow and attain success.

A start-up business can be the riskiest Plan B model because of the high failure rate, therefore this chapter is essential to help you evaluate your ideas *before* you write a check or borrow money. The necessary analysis may seem like drudgery compared to the excitement of actually setting things in motion, but you will save a significant amount of time and money in the long run. Adopt the mantra of *ready...aim, aim, aim...fire!*

Starting a New Business

Since this is the *real deal guide,* I will give you both the good and the bad news about starting your own business. The *good news* is that starting a business is not actually all that hard to do. Access to the tools for starting a business has never been easier. The Internet has made local and global reach a breeze, and it's instantly available to those who know how to tap into it. You can go online and get a domain name, create a website, register with the authorities, get the permits and—*BOOM!*—you are in business. When you analyze and do your homework on your business idea—which is in keeping with the *ready...aim, aim, aim...fire!* mantra—you will go deeper into the *what, who, why,* and *how* questions that will ultimately determine your Plan B business' success.

The *bad news* is that approximately 80% of start-ups fail within their first three years.[1] This may be the riskiest of the four ways to create a Plan B. And by *risk,* I mean not only a failed business, but also the lost time and money you have invested in it. It is not uncommon for business start-ups to take up to three years or longer before they become profitable. That means you will have to have the money to pay your personal bills as well as those of the business. The No. 1 reason most start-up businesses fail is because they are underfunded. So do the up-front analysis I suggest, and you will greatly improve your odds of success.

Two Types of Start-Up Businesses

Basically, start-up businesses are one of two types: a **duplication,** which is defined as doing something that's already been done, or an **innovation,** which is defined as doing something new. *Duplication* is pretty straightforward because you are imitating a business that is usually well defined, and almost all of the mistakes have already been made. To survive, you need to be at least as good as your competition, as perceived by your customer. To succeed, you must surpass your competitors.

Duplication

Let's look at one common start-up idea in the *duplication* genre:

> Victoria, a Cordon Bleu-trained chef, justified her recent shift from frustrating employment to frantic entrepreneurship. "There comes a point in a mountain climber's life when they want to climb Mount Everest. And there comes a point in a chef's life when they want to open their own restaurant.
>
> "For me, that was a little over two years ago. I had been working for other people for about ten years and I was dying to do something new with vegetarian food. I was tired of working really, really hard for other people who *didn't* work really, really hard.
>
> "A friend said to me, 'You've opened so many restaurants for other people that opening your own will be a piece of cake.' I decided to open The Harvest Kitchen, where I could specialize in vegetarian recipes and use fresh, local produce whenever possible.
>
> "My friend turned out to be right. I knew what was coming and, as a result, I knew what needed to be done. One method I used was to find a coach to help keep me on track—someone who had started, run, and sold several successful restaurants.
>
> "It wasn't easy, but I had made it work for other restaurant owners, and I have now made it work

for me too. It's been two years and I've developed a loyal following and created media buzz. And we are making money!"

Restaurants are a dime a dozen, but what has made Victoria's successful is a heaping plateful of the Six Key Ingredients from chapter 6. Specifically, she had market trends in her favor, a strong partnership with a coach, and a unique offering.

Innovation

The *innovation* path to a start-up business is much less obvious and usually much more convoluted than duplicating something that has already been done. There are many paths to success in innovation. There are, however, the common threads in almost all innovative new businesses: someone had the time, the determination, and an idea on how to solve an irritating problem. And if it was irritating to that person, perhaps it was irritating other people enough that it was worthwhile to create a business that solves that particular problem.

Here are two examples of innovation as a new business.

When Debbie Meyer was a child, her mother would not let her eat cake at events because the server often sliced the cake and used a finger to balance the piece while serving it. After placing the cake on a plate, the server would lick the frosting off her finger and then go on to serve the next piece. When Debbie became a mom herself, she solved this messy, unhygienic problem by inventing and patenting her first product, the Debbie Meyer kakekut'rs. This utensil cuts and serves the cake without it ever touching the server's hands. Debbie designed two shapes; one for round cakes, one for sheet cakes.

Her product was launched on the QVC shopping channel and sold at the astonishing rate of over $30,000 per minute. She sold all 10,000 units of stock in a few short minutes. Today, this product is sold worldwide and solves a problem millions of people have identified in their own lives.

Debbie has solved many household problems by inventing and developing a range of products that make life easier and more organized, and that save money.

One big problem she has tackled is the amount of fresh fruits and vegetables most households waste because they go bad before they are used. Debbie set out to learn what causes this rapid spoilage and how to slow it down. The solution was her Debbie Meyer GreenBags. They're made with a natural mineral that creates a beneficial environment inside the bag and slows the spoiling process. Debbie has sold more than 600 million of these amazing bags on TV shopping channels, at retail stores, through her infomercials and website. She continues to create products that solve problems and has actually created a market segment that did not exist before: food storage that actively works to keep its contents fresh.[2]

At other times, innovation is simply the result of serendipity blended with consistent follow-through, which is illustrated by our second example of an innovative start-up business.

Lonnie Johnson was an aerospace engineer working with NASA. One of the projects he worked on was an environmentally friendly heat pump that used water instead of Freon. One day to test this pet project, he aimed the nozzle into his bathtub, pulled the lever, and blasted a powerful stream of water straight into it.

Lonnie's immediate reaction was, "That is awesome!"

He soon developed the prototype for what we now know as the Super Soaker, a high-powered water gun used by kids and adults alike. After seven more years of tinkering and tireless sales-pitching, Lonnie finally caught the interest of the Larami Corporation, who told him to set up a meeting when he was in town. But they warned him not to make a special trip. Despite that, Lonnie made the trip, they liked what they saw, bought it, and put it into mass production. The Super Soaker was vastly superior to previous generations of squirt guns, and quickly became one of the most popular toys in the world. It has held its ranking among the world's top twenty best-selling toys every year since its creation. The total sales are more than a billion dollars, and Lonnie's royalties are estimated to be more than $20 million.[3]

> Have a plan. Follow the plan, and you'll be surprised how successful you can be. Most people don't have a plan. That's why it's easy to beat most folks.
>
> —PAUL "BEAR" BRYANT, FOOTBALL COACH, UNIVERSITY OF ALABAMA

So, what made it happen for Debbie Meyer and Lonnie Johnson? Luck? Skill? Creativity? A willingness to keep going? Probably yes to all of those, but we also have to factor in a lot of manufacturing and sales calculations, and many hours of planning. Add a generous dollop of good timing and stir in a healthy measure of perseverance.

Plan Bs generally don't happen by accident, hence the use of the word *plan*.

The Real Deal Checklist

It's finally time to take a close look at the powerful Real Deal Checklist I created to help you determine the viability of your business idea. By finding the answers to each of the checklist items, you can identify where your idea is strong and competitive and where you may need to spend more time finding answers.

Each of the six areas explores a different aspect of your business idea. You may not know all of the answers right away, but you will want to have them before you actually launch your start-up.

To help you see how to use the Real Deal Checklist, we will apply each section's items to the idea of starting a consulting company. Take a few minutes now to read through the checklist and familiarize yourself with its components. Then we'll get busy using it.

For each business idea you have, go through the checklist and follow the steps. For example, if you have three ideas for starting a business, you will create three separate sets of responses.

THE REAL DEAL CHECKLIST

1. <u>WHAT</u>	Develop a list of what you want to create or resell—your product or services. Make sure they are: • Practical, i.e., useful, with a wide number of applications • Immediately useable • Able to withstand the competition in the marketplace • Visual, in that you can touch them or easily understand their benefits
2. <u>WHO</u>	Identify your target market of buyers and users to verify you know who this is. Make sure you know such information as: • How you will market and sell to them • Where they are located: within a few miles of your business, within the same city or state, elsewhere in the nation, or even international • How much they will buy from you at one time • How often they will buy more • Ensure your target market is growing, or at least stable, and preferably not shrinking
3. <u>WHY</u>	Determine why others will want, need, and buy your product or services by identifying the: • Benefits of what you offer • Pain that it will ease or eliminate • Pleasure it will bring now or in the future • Trends that will help or hurt your offerings
4. <u>HOW</u>	Decide how you will fulfill your offerings to your buyers: • From online/Internet orders your customers place (usually faster and cheaper) • From in-person orders (offers the highest relationship satisfaction but is more costly and takes more time) • Hire employees or outsource work to another company • Store and deliver your product offerings yourself or outsource your warehousing, shipping, and delivery
5. <u>MORE</u>	Create ways to expand your offerings: • Offer free, low-, and moderate-priced products or services to introduce people to you and ease them into becoming customers…then up-sell them to higher priced offerings • Franchising • Licensing • Wholesale • Retail • Technology • Mobile apps (downloadable applications)
6. <u>YOU</u>	Identify your roles and responsibilities, so you are clear on what you will and will not do in the business: • How you will work in your areas of expertise and strengths • What skills and knowledge you are missing • How to accommodate your lack of skills or knowledge for such tasks as sales, finances, and/or operations

As we work through each area in this powerful checklist, you will see how it can help you determine whether or not to pursue any business idea. For example, many seasoned professionals decide to become consultants when their Plan A is no longer working for them or is not a viable option anymore. Consulting is a low-cost start-up, since you can use your expertise, work from a home office, and begin working on this Plan B part-time while still at a Plan A job.

The Real Deal Checklist helps you decide if your ideas are worth pursuing—or to realize they won't be successful. By doing this work in advance, you can avoid the famous last words of so many devastated would-be entrepreneurs, "Well, it seemed like a good idea at the time."

To see how the Real Deal Checklist works in real life, here is how a client of mine used the checklist to evaluate and expand her idea to start a consulting and training company.

> Sometimes you have to go slow to go fast. You need to create a solid base and a plan before you start building. Once it is in place, you can go fast.
>
> —KATHLEEN RICH-NEW, BUSINESS CONSULTANT, SPEAKER, EXECUTIVE COACH, CLARITY WORKS CONSULTING; AUTHOR, *PLAN B*

Kate is in her late forties and has a quality and project-management background working with large, complex, and confidential projects in the aviation industry for government contactors. She has a knack for getting poorly behaving groups to create a common vision and work together to complete projects. Specifically, she brings both the hard, technical skills and the soft skills (i.e., influence, facilitation, and cooperation) to each project so team members can figure out how to get the job done.

She knew her company's government contract would end in three years, and there was no option to renew. Since Kate was too young to consider retiring, she asked me to work with her to create her Plan B. She is still working full-time at her Plan A job but has decided to look into starting her own business on a part-time basis.

Kate wants to use her expertise to offer consulting and training to help companies more efficiently and effectively manage project implementation. She is also considering offering soft-skills training to project managers and teams that need to gain the cooperation of people who aren't happy about upcoming changes related to the project.

Let's apply the Real Deal Checklist to Kate's Plan B to see how it works. First, we will look at *what* Kate has to offer buyers.

1. __WHAT__	Develop a list of what you want to create or resell— your product or services. Make sure they are:
	• Practical, i.e., useful, with a wide number of applications • Immediately useable • Able to withstand the competition in the marketplace • Visual, in that you can touch them or easily understand their benefits

Kate is considering offering these products and services:

Products: Training via the classroom, webinars, and DVDs/CDs with workbooks. She can use assessments to identify the skills and behaviors of the members of the project teams to determine if they are the right mix. She is considering creating her own certification in Project Behavior Management. Kate plans to write newsletters, expert articles, and eventually books.

Services: The scope of Kate's offerings can include pre-project audits, strategic coaching, project-crisis problem solving, project-team selection, and post-project debriefs and assessments. She wants to offer small group and one-on-one coaching for those who lead project-implementation teams. She can develop and deliver monthly teleseminars addressing common failures in project management. Kate has considered creating a membership association for project managers with an annual conference. She can also offer expert consulting for oversight and advice on critical projects.

Kate has created an impressive list of products and services. Now she needs to evaluate how desirable they are. In the interest of time, we will focus mainly on evaluating the services—and not the products—Kate wants to offer.

The first bullet in the *What* section of the check-list asks how *practical* Kate's services would be. Since delayed or failed projects are expensive for any organization, her business idea (to help clients avoid this expense) is of good quality. She would work with project managers and with specific departments, such as IT and engineering. The number of *applications* is limited to project implementation, but large companies regularly have expensive projects they want to be successful so there may be a big demand for her services.

Kate's offerings will be within the project management niche, which is very specific but can be applied to any industry. Her services are *immediately useable,* since she can personally jump in and get an organization's projects back on track. She can also design her training to align with the Project Management Institute (PMI) training and certification programs.

Kate's research found that there are not any other training organizations specializing in addressing the soft skills or people issues, so it currently appears there are no *competitors*. Her training and consulting services have clear *benefits* that can save large companies millions of dollars, and months or years of time. For example, think about how many times you have read about projects being years late and millions of dollars over budget.

For the *What* section of the checklist, the services in Kate's plan look solid. They are practical because customers can save substantial time and money, and it appears there are no competitors.

Next, Kate determined *who* her buyers will be:

2. <u>WHO</u>	Identify your target market of buyers and users to verify you know who this is. Make sure you know such information as:
	• How you will market and sell to them • Where they are located: within a few miles of your business, within the same city or state, elsewhere in the nation, or even international • How much they will buy from you at one time • How often they will buy more • Ensure your target market is growing, or at least stable, and preferably not shrinking

The second area analyzes Kate's target market of *buyers*. She has *identified* large organizations with multi-million-dollar projects because they have the money to buy her services and enough *pain* to take action. Her research says that Chief Executive Officers (CEOs) and Chief Information Officers (CIOs) are the primary decision makers who buy this type of service. Their top concerns reflect the common issue of potential costly delays with project implementation.

Kate is focusing on the people side of project management in large organizations as a unique business niche. In addition, any profession that has regular project-implementation requirements is a potential target for her.

To *market and sell* to her primary target buyers of CEOs and CIOs, Kate can identify the publications they read and get articles published in them. She could become a speaker for the industry conferences they attend. Kate can contact her former bosses and associates to tell them about her new business and ask for referrals.

Kate can also identify training companies that already have project management programs that do not include soft-skills training, and then offer to partner with them. She will determine if there are certification agencies who may be interested in adding her training to their programs.

Her clients can be *located* anywhere in the world, but she has decided to develop her business in the United States first, because she already has contacts here.

How much her clients will *buy* from Kate at any *one time* will vary. Clients could be buying both her consulting services and training. She will only work on a few projects at one time, so her plan has some limitations that are directly tied to her availability. Kate can create additional sales by selling her training to her current consulting customers as well as other companies.

How often they will buy also varies. By targeting large companies, Kate may have several consulting assignments within the same company. For training, there will be a constant flow of clients through the Project Management Institute (PMI) as people pursue their project-management certification. In addition, big companies can send a large number of their employees to her training. If Kate develops advanced courses, she would have repeat customers.

The last bullet point in the *Who* section of the checklist helps Kate realize her target market is *stable,* and her business could grow to quite a large size as she is able to contract with several large companies, government agencies, and government contractors. Kate has been attending conferences and meetings to talk with project managers from other countries and has confirmed that project-implementation problems are the same in the United States, Saudi Arabia, or Spain, for example. As a result, Kate can decide to move into the international markets after she has achieved success in the United States.

In summary, Kate's target market is specific and large enough to be very profitable. Both the product and service offerings of the business will provide a steady stream of customers. Her plan continues to be solid.

Now we will see *why* people will want to buy what Kate can offer.

The third area of the checklist evaluates *why* someone will want to buy what you offer.

3. <u>WHY</u>	Determine why others will want, need, and buy your product or services by identifying the:
	<ul><li>Benefits of what you offer</li><li>Pain that it will ease or eliminate</li><li>Pleasure it will bring now or in the future</li><li>Needs that exist and are not being met</li><li>Trends that will help or hurt your offerings</li></ul>

In Kate's business model, people want to buy her products and services because of Kate herself. She has firsthand knowledge from her twenty-plus years of working with teams to solve the problems and *ease the pain* resulting from failing projects. She has seen the millions of dollars wasted when large projects are delayed by uncooperative departments, team members who can't get along with each other, and when teams do not have the right mix of skills.

She's very aware of *current needs* in her marketplace. Kate has been networking with project managers, visiting Internet chat rooms, and participating in project-management forums to verify there continues to be a high level of frustration and concern with the lack of soft skills in project teams. One organization told her they would hire her as soon as she launches her new company. They already see the *benefits* of bringing her in to get their project back on track—a project that's already cost them more than $300,000 and thousands of lost hours of work.

Kate's experience and research has shown most projects fail because they were badly planned, had poor soft skills, or had work teams with competing agendas. By using the Real Deal Checklist and other resources, she has developed additional assessment models to identify clients' core issue(s) and the options to resolve them. Kate's experience is extensive, so she is well qualified to offer this type of consulting and training.

Thus, it's clear that organizations can use her consulting and training services. Her services can *benefit* organizations by saving them time and money, and by helping to eliminate the *pain* of delayed or failed projects. Her clients might not derive as much pleasure from her training and consulting as they would if she were providing surfing lessons, for example, but achieving goals and finishing projects on time—or earlier—and under budget is certainly rewarding and pleasurable. The *needs* for well-implemented projects are universal; and there are not other providers with similar offerings that are meeting the needs of organizations that lack soft-skills training.

Market trends appear to be stable because large companies will always have complex and expensive projects that need to be implemented on time and within budget. On the other hand, her business could be impacted by a down economy when businesses delay projects and spending. Government agencies and contractors are a target market for Kate, and cuts in government spending could impact her business through a slow down in sales. But it could also increase her business because failed projects are highly visible with more serious consequences.

Since there appears to be no current competitors, now is a good time for Kate to launch both her consulting and training services.

Based on our evaluation, we know *why* organizations will buy what Kate plans to offer and how it will help them. Her business idea continues to be viable.

Next, Kate examined *how* she will deliver her offerings to her customers.

4. **HOW**	Decide how you will fulfill your offerings to your buyers:
	• From online/Internet orders your customers place (usually faster and cheaper)
	• From in-person orders (offers the highest relationship satisfaction but is more costly and takes more time)
	• Hire employees or outsource work to another company
	• Store and deliver your product offerings yourself or outsource your warehousing, shipping, and delivery

As a consultant, Kate will initially be personally involved in all of the projects. As the demand for consulting work increases, she has decided to hire *independent contractors* to help her with the workload. She will delay *hiring employees* until the customer base and demands are great enough.

She can provide the training to her clients *in person,* delivered via the Internet, or presented by other trainers. Kate can also record her training sessions and create CDs and DVDs to sell. She can outsource the ordering of CDs and DVDs and their production and shipping.

Kate's answers to the *How* section of the Real Deal Checklist are straightforward. She will require little infrastructure in the beginning, since she will not need such things as facilities, recording studios, warehouses, or employees.

The fifth section of the checklist, called *More,* provides ideas on how to expand what is currently offered to customers.

5. __MORE__	Create ways to expand your offerings:
	• Offer free, low-, and moderate-priced products or services to introduce people to you and ease them into becoming customers…then up-sell them to higher priced offerings
	• Franchising • Licensing
	• Wholesale • Retail
	• Technology • Mobile apps (downloadable applications)

Since Kate plans to establish herself as the expert in soft-skills training for project management teams, she will create multiple products and training programs available for sale. Kate's plan is very rich in this area; it has numerous options.

In an effort to bring potential customers to her, Kate might start by offering a *free* newsletter to her target customers; she might also provide articles for other publications, and offer webinars. She can then create a *low-priced product* to sell for about $100, then a moderately priced item for around $500 and higher-priced products for more than $1,000. She can continue to develop new products at different prices to create buyers at multiple levels. These products can be sold without her personal involvement, which creates a passive income stream.

Franchising could eventually be an option after Kate has achieved a solid level of success and name recognition. Franchisees would offer the same training she delivers. Franchising would require Kate to develop the infrastructure of support systems, financial reporting, operations, sales, and marketing models. Kate could charge a one-time and/or renewable franchising fee and collect royalties on her materials. (See chapter 9 for more specific information about franchises.)

Licensing may be a better option for Kate in a few years. She could license her training, assessments, and processes to other trainers to use with their clients. And she could charge a one-time and/or renewable licensing fee to the other trainers, who would also buy and use her materials that would pay her royalties.

Kate can also sell her products wholesale to other organizations that sell to project managers, such as associations, online book stores, and large companies. (This option depends on her ability to develop products and materials that others will find valuable, of course.) Kate can also sell her products directly from her website and at speeches and conferences. The *retail* model of selling her products in stores does not appear to work for Kate's products at this point.

Technology works well for Kate's business. Her plan is to create a website with online assessments, member chat rooms, and forums. Downloadable webinars and teleseminars are also part of what she can offer.

Kate can work *remotely* with clients via conference calls or Skype. She can also do radio interviews via telephone. Television interviews can be done in local affiliate television stations that can be aired nationally.

Kate has some ideas about how *mobile apps* (downloadable applications) would work with her products. For example, she could convert her project-problem assessment into one that project managers can access and use from a smart phone or iPad. She can also provide guidelines on how to resolve conflicts of competing agendas or issues of non-performance by the team members. This could be a very powerful way to provide immediate help to project teams in trouble.

Kate's plan continues to be promising in the *More* section of the Real Deal Checklist. She has a lot of options for expanding her offerings and increasing revenue.

Kate then moved on to determining what her roles and responsibilities will and will not be as she analyzed the *You* section of the checklist.

6. <u>YOU</u>	Identify your roles and responsibilities, so you are clear on what you will and will not do in the business: • How you will work in your areas of expertise and strengths • What skills and knowledge you are missing • How to accommodate your lack of skills or knowledge for such tasks as sales, finances, and/or operations

The sixth and last section of the checklist uses the work you did in chapter 5, when you identified your work lifestyle. Kate knows her *expertise* comes from her experience and understanding of making project teams work. She is comfortable meeting with senior executives to help them identify their problems and work together to create solutions. Kate knows what her expertise is and where her *strengths* lie.

Kate determined she needs to find others who can provide such services as marketing, IT, web design and support, fulfillment, and bookkeeping and payroll services, for example. She recognizes that she needs a partner to develop the curriculum for her training, and also others who can teach it. She knows she needs help with sales and plans to find people already selling to her target customers. In the early stages of her Plan B business, she has decided it's better to find contractors who can deliver those services to her. Adding employees too early can be a cash drain if not enough paying customers are in place yet.

Let's review what Kate and I found as we worked through each of the six sections in the Real Deal Checklist.

Overall, Kate's idea for a consulting and training company that works with project implementation teams is strong. We discovered that she has the potential to be a go-to expert, since no one else is providing the soft-skills training or consulting that she will. It appears that the products and materials Kate can create will generate significant income, but it will take Kate time to develop them. She already has potential customers because of her contacts from her previous employers and associates. One potential pitfall that needs to be addressed is getting through the noise barrier and gate keepers that surround her C-level buyers. (C-level refers to executive titles that begin with a C, such as CEO, COO, and CFO.) Kate already has ideas about how to connect with her target buyers, and she is a very resourceful and persistent person.

Since she is still working in her Plan A job, she may be able to offer her services to her current employer after she leaves. She has some of the skills she needs for her Plan B business and has identified the areas in which she needs help from others.

Do you see how you can determine if your start-up business idea is strong enough to succeed? It does take a lot of work to get to this point, but if you decide your idea is strong and you are now going to start working on it—celebrate! If you find that your idea is not strong enough—celebrate that too! You will know if more work will improve your idea or if you need to find another one. You have saved yourself years of work and frustration, and a lot of money.

You are starting a Plan B business to make money, and carefully working through the Real Deal Checklist will show you how you can. It helps ensure you are one of the successful 20% of start-ups that remain in business.

We'll continue to use the Real Deal Checklist and apply it to the other three Plan B options so you can see how to best use it in those situations.

Wrap Up

You have learned the good and bad news about starting a business, as well as the advantages and disadvantages.

And you know more about the two types of start-up businesses: duplication and innovation.

You experienced the Real Deal Checklist as we applied it to Kate's consulting idea to help companies manage project implementation more efficiently and effectively. By honestly completing even just the checklist, you should significantly increase your start-up's chance of success.

Next, in chapter 8, you will learn the good and bad news and the advantages and disadvantages associated with buying a business. We will apply the Six Key Ingredients from chapter 6—as well as the Real Deal Checklist from this chapter—toward the purchase of a tanning salon. We'll cover the best ways to learn more about businesses for sale, as well as how to find, evaluate, and use business brokers. I will introduce the process of due diligence and show how it is a crucial step in buying a company.

Follow me now to the next page, where we'll uncover the secrets to successfully buying an existing business instead of starting one...

Notes

1   Lou Vescio
    Certified Business Intermediary (CBI)
    Coastal Business Intermediaries, Inc., Melbourne, FL
    www.agencybrokerageconsultants.com

2   Debbie Meyer
    www.debbiemeyer.com

3   Lonnie Johnson
    How I Made My Millions, CNBC
    www.cnbc.com

CHAPTER 8

The Real Deal about Buying a Business

YOU MAY BE THINKING, "Why should I reinvent the wheel to come up with a new Plan B? There are existing businesses for sale that are already making money."

And you are correct. Someone had an idea and figured out how to make it work, and now you can take advantage of their success.

This is the second of four chapters that take an in-depth look at the different ways to create a Plan B. This chapter guides you through the tasks you will need to do *before* you buy a business. You will learn how to conduct a search to buy an existing business, how to complete additional due diligence, and what to expect during the buying process.

You have already completed a personal version of due diligence on yourself from the work you have done in chapters 2 and 5. Doing that type of due diligence puts you in a stronger position to have a successful business.

Other people who haven't carefully examined their own motivation and taken a hard look at their own skills will be at a decided disadvantage.

Buying a business is pretty straightforward, but it can be a lot like buying a used car; the owner will usually do everything possible to make the business look as bright, shiny, and attractive as possible. Therefore, you need to understand what is required to conduct your due diligence research. Quite honestly, you will spend most of your time analyzing financial information and requiring the seller to prove everything he or she says about the business is accurate, and there is very specific information later in this chapter about how to accomplish this successfully and thoroughly. Your overall job is to look behind the curtains and under the rug, so to speak. I definitely advise you to enlist the help of experts, typically business brokers and bankers, with this process. They know what to look for and how to evaluate the data.

To get started, let's look at one buyer who could have used what you are about to learn.

What Happens When You Ignore the Experts, the Resources, and the Information?

This story is typical of the problems that occur when emotions and impulse take the place of hard facts and systematic analysis. Meet Paul, a young professional who was a former graduate student of mine.

> Paul, a mechanical engineer, was in frantic search mode after being laid off by a large manufacturing company. He was frustrated because the only responses his job hunt yielded were

for jobs requiring him to relocate. Paul did not want to move away from his family and friends, so he started looking for a Plan B.

Below is one of my conversations with Paul. As you read, you will better understand the pros and cons of Paul's plan because of the work you have already done.

"I have a chance to buy a tanning salon," Paul explained, practically breathless with excitement. "It's really busy and it's making a lot of money. The owner has been playing cat-and-mouse games with me on the price. It seems like a great deal. I really think I have to jump in now, or he may change his mind again and decide not to sell it at all. I just don't want to miss the chance."

"That's great, Paul," I said, "and which attorney are you using? Also, who is helping you complete the due diligence on the business? Have you run this by your CPA or your banker? Are you using a broker? They could help you determine the accurate business valuation so you are not overpaying." I could see that Paul was headed full speed for the edge of the cliff, and I hoped to at least slow him down so he could more clearly see where he was going.

"I don't want to waste the money on accountants or lawyers, and there isn't enough time to consult with a broker. This is a simple buying agreement and the bank is not involved. My family is providing the cash to buy it," Paul said.

I worked hard to convince him to rethink his strategy. "You have no idea how many ways you can find yourself upside down in a business if you have not used experts. They know what to look for and how to value a business. Sellers lie all the time about how profitable their business is. If you are not using experts, then be prepared to lose all of your investment and possibly more."

I could see that my counsel was falling on deaf ears. Paul was too consumed by his own enthusiasm for the idea. He closed the deal two weeks later.

My sincere hope was that the business would work out for Paul but the odds were against him, not only because he was too emotional about the purchase but also because he had not completed very much of the necessary due diligence.

Three years later, he struggles to keep his doors open. He blames everything on the downturn in the economy. I reminded him that I had asked, "Paul, don't you think that when people lose their jobs, getting a tan becomes an unnecessary luxury?" He didn't remember that particular conversation. Eager buyers often have blind spots.

Paul also dismissed our discussion of industry research that linked the increase of skin cancer to tanning beds. He did not take time to understand the overall industry trends or use them to evaluate the business.

Sadly, Paul is representative of far too many people who don't know how to determine if buying a specific business is a good decision.

So that you don't fall into the same situation as Paul did, let's apply the valuable Six Key Ingredients from chapter 6 and the Real Deal Checklist from chapter 7 to Paul's decision to buy the tanning salon. You will see where he made mistakes and you, at least, can learn from them.

First of all, Paul never determined if the tanning salon was the right business for him—which he would have known if he had done the work in chapter 2. He did not know how to think through the business, as detailed in chapter 5. Nor did he understand the Six Key Ingredients of most successful businesses from chapter 6. He also refused to get experts to guide him toward a better buying decision.

However, you already hold the tools to make a good buying decision, and you are smart enough to slow down and use your available resources. If Paul had just taken the time to Google "tanning salon industry trends," he might have seen a few things to give him pause in his headlong rush to become a business owner of this particular company. Basic research like using Google is a great place to start your due diligence.

Buying a Business 101, and More

Continuing with my promise to provide a *real deal guide* for your Plan B, we'll discuss the good and bad news about buying a business.

The good news is that buying a successful business is inherently less risky than starting your own. The business already has customers and products or services that people want. The processes are in place, and the sales and marketing efforts are working.

The bad news is that even though the business is profitable now, there may be economic trends, new products, or technology that will impact the business' success later. Current customers may use a change in ownership as a reason to shop around for a new provider. Or key employees may quit and open a competing business. Fortunately, you can evaluate these and other risks by using the tools you have already learned and the new information in this chapter.

Also, because I'm committed to providing you with the best possible advice for your Plan B decision, let's also look at the advantages and disadvantages of buying a business.

Advantages and Disadvantages of Buying a Business

Let me introduce you to Lou Vescio, a serial entrepreneur and certified business broker who ensures his business buyers make smart decisions.[1]

Lou has a diverse background, starting with a twenty-year career as an Air Force aviator. Following the military, he joined Texas Instruments and held a variety of managerial positions, including manufacturing, engineering, production control, operations analysis, and product marketing.

Lou began developing his entrepreneurial skills when he and his wife, Maggie, started Futurekids of Virginia Beach, a franchised computer-training business that grew to one of the top five franchises in the country within its first year. At the same time he was growing Futurekids, Lou cofounded ICTS, Inc., a high-end computer-training business. This business grew to $11.5 million in sales in its first five years.

After Lou sold both businesses in the years 2000 and 2001, he enjoyed a short retirement, and then joined Ferrari Sunbelt Business Brokers in Florida. During his first year, he was the top sales associate in the company's five area offices. Lou became licensed in two of the Sunbelt territories and became one of the top fifty business brokers in the Sunbelt Business Brokers Network, Inc., which consisted of more than 300 offices in the United States and twenty-five foreign countries at the time.

Impressed yet?

Me too, and that's why I want you to learn from Lou about buying a business. He now owns his own business brokerage practice, Coastal Business Intermediaries, Inc., which specializes in high-end business brokerage and lower-middle-market merger and acquisition transactions in the one- to twenty-million-dollar range. Lou also acts as a consultant for the local Small Business Administration (SBA) Business Development Center, which offers free consulting and low-cost classes for buyers and sellers.

Here's what Lou says about the *advantages* of buying an existing business:

- When you buy an existing business, it already has a provable track record of customers, sales, and profitability. It's provable because you can perform due diligence on the company's financial records, tax returns, and customer and supplier records.
- An existing company has built a client base. The processes to attract and retain customers have been figured out, so you can continue what has already been created and add your own ideas too.

- There is already an existing infrastructure of processes, products, marketing, sales, delivery, employees, and location. You don't have to figure it out, and it is always easier to improve something that already exists.
- The business should provide you with immediate cash flow. Confirm this by reviewing such records such as tax returns, profit and loss statements, accounts receivable, invoicing, and inventory.
- The business should provide you with a Return on Investment (ROI), which means you will make a profit on your total investment (i.e., the price you pay for the business). The ROI formula evaluates the efficiency of an investment, which is a critical determination. If you are going to spend money, you want to get your original investment back, and hopefully a big profit.[2]
- The business should provide a Return on Invested Capital (ROIC). Invested capital is your down payment, closing costs, and initial operating capital. The ROIC measures how well the company generates a return, based on the initial investment. The ROIC is calculated as a percentage.[3]
- If you can, find a business that qualifies for a Small Business Administration (SBA) loan. The lending bank will conduct additional due diligence, and the bankers won't make the loan if they believe the investment is too risky.
- Keep in mind that 90% of resale businesses with cash flow greater than $100,000 will still be operating more than five years after the sale.

There are also *disadvantages* and several reasons to be cautious when buying a business:

> "Ninety percent of all resold businesses with cash flows greater than $100,000 will still be operating more than five years after the sale."
>
> – LOU VESCIO, COASTAL BUSINESS INTERMEDIARIES, INC.[1]

- Most businesses listed for sale have poor financial documentation, so it may be difficult to get an accurate picture of the company's profitability. This is why you must conduct your own due diligence and analyze all of the available records. The seller must prove to you the accuracy of what he or she is claiming.

- Just like someone selling a car or house that has problems, business sellers and, unfortunately, some business brokers are so desperate to make the sale that they sometimes lie. You need to have your own experts help you evaluate all aspects of the business. (There are specific guidelines for using business brokers later in this chapter.)

- Trust only what is on the tax return as you verify the business's financial data during your due diligence. You can dig, audit, and analyze, but in the end, the business tax returns will be your most accurate measurement. Tax evasion carries serious consequences so, for that reason, be sure to get the tax returns directly from the Internal Revenue Service (IRS). It is fairly easy to create a tax return that looks real, so don't be fooled by anything that doesn't come from the IRS.

- Avoid businesses where the owner does not report cash transactions because that means there are other things the owner is hiding. For example, the owner may say that the business has an extra $50,000 in cash sales, but he or she can't prove it. Besides, if the business owner lies to the IRS, do you think they might be lying to you too?

- In the current market, less than 3% of existing businesses that are for sale will qualify for an SBA loan because of the program's increasingly strict requirements. SBA loans have historically been processed in ninety days; now it is taking up to five months in some cases.

- Only about 10% of businesses offered for sale will actually sell. If the seller is using high-pressure tactics, such as saying other buyers are lined up, or that the offer is only good for a few days, it could be true, but—statistically—it's not.

Applying What You Have Learned

Let's circle back to Paul's decision to buy the tanning salon, and apply what you have learned. How much it would have helped Paul if he had asked himself even some of the questions you now know to ask!

First, we will apply the Six Key Ingredients from chapter 6.

- *Market trends:* No, the tanning salon business trends are not in his favor. Major layoffs in the local area had been announced. The salon is located where a large number of the affected employees live. Also, the community was not growing when Paul bought the business, and it was projected to actually shrink as laid-off employees moved to take jobs in other locations. Lastly, the link between tanning beds and skin cancer is an ominous factor. The advent of new, spray-on tanning products without the cancer link should have been another warning signal.
- *Consumable products or ongoing services:* Yes, this ingredient is present because maintaining a tan clearly requires return visits. Tanning beds are faster and provide a more even tan than does lying in the sun. However, if money is short, people are more likely to remember that lying in the sun is

free and a viable, readily available substitute…so maybe Paul gets only partial credit here for this key ingredient.

- *Perfect timing:* This ingredient could go either way, because timing factors into Paul's business in more than one way. First of all, the demands for tans are seasonal, with the highest traffic in the spring and summer. Paul bought the business in March, so the tanning season was just beginning. However, the long-term timing was not good due to the upcoming layoffs.

- *Strong compensation or attractive margins:* The attractive margins ingredient earns a yes. It is a profitable business, as shown by the tax records. The salon also offers retail products at a 300% markup. Paul's compensation is tied directly to the number of customers he attracts and retains, so that's somewhat up in the air.

- *Powerful partnerships:* The business has a few partnerships that create customers. A nearby fitness center refers its members to the salon. The salon has an established reputation with the local high schools, which has historically led to a jump in sales during prom season, spring break, and summer vacation. Unfortunately, none of these partnerships are considered powerful. So, again, only a partial credit goes to Paul.

- *Unique products or exclusive technology:* Neither of those key ingredients is found here. The tanning beds are readily available, as are the new spray tans.

In so far as the Six Key Ingredients go, Paul has in his favor the attractive margins for the business, and the half-credit each for ongoing consumable services and for partnerships. The demand is seasonal, not year-round, which creates peaks and valleys. He will certainly need cash reserves for his off months.

The primary ingredient not working in Paul's favor is the market trends. The fact that massive layoffs were scheduled within the next thirteen months should have immediately squelched his decision to buy the salon. Also, the seasonal nature of the tanning business should have been carefully analyzed month by month and would have shown up as a red flag. There is nothing unique about Paul's products or technology, and substitutes are easily found.

So it looks like Paul's tanning salon has only partial credit for two key ingredients out of the six.

Now let's use the Real Deal Checklist and apply it to Paul's tanning salon.

- *What:* The desire to look suntanned is well known and the key to this business. A tanning salon is *practical;* it will create the results the buyer is looking for, and it is easier for a customer to spend a few minutes on a tanning bed when it's convenient, rather than hours lying outside at a potentially inconvenient time. It is *immediately useable* in that all someone has to do is sign up and start tanning; the results appear instantly. There is only one *application* for a tanning salon's offering—to get a tan. And because the results are *visual,* customers understand and appreciate the *benefits.* On the other hand, if a competing salon opened, Paul could lose customers and may not be able to withstand much *competition.* Also, because the salon products are readily available online at a reduced price, *repeat purchases* at the salon may be weak.

- *Who:* The business has established customers who are *located* within a seven-mile radius; some are up to fifteen miles away. Paul should determine how many of the current customers will be affected by the upcoming layoffs and how to attract new customers. Customers typically *buy* tanning packages that expire in six months, or they buy a monthly membership with unlimited tanning sessions. It is common for new customers to *buy a variety of products* to accelerate the tanning process and to remain tan longer. The *profile* of the tanning salon customer varies according to age, gender, race, and income. The demographics, however, are easier to determine: between age sixteen and forty-five, female, Caucasian, middle class, and with a disposable income. The *target market* may shrink due to layoffs, and the community itself may shrink too.

- *Why:* Looking and feeling good are the *benefit* and the *pleasure* customers experience. The *pains* being resolved by a tanning bed are tan lines and embarrassingly pale skin. These *needs* are superficial, yes, but emotionally charged for some consumers. The *trends* that could hurt the salon are the upcoming layoffs and the link between skin cancer and tanning beds.

- *How:* Customers will have to come into the tanning salon *in person* for their tans. Products can be *purchased* at the salon or ordered on the salon *website*. Personalizing each *customer service experience* will be one of the solutions to attracting and retaining more clients.

- *More:* A tanning salon has limited *expansion* options. Paul does not have the business experience or financial resources to *expand* his one and only tanning salon. However, he could add a spray-tanning option. If the demographics work well, he could also consider adding a nail technician or a masseuse.

- *You:* Paul did not do the work you did in chapters 2 and 5 because this book had not yet been written. However, knowing Paul, he still wouldn't have made use of this resource because he clearly wanted to own and run his own business. With his sense of great urgency, he was blind to his *weaknesses* and unaware of all the *skills he needed* to run the business.

By using the Real Deal Checklist, the analysis reveals the tanning salon had some positives; however, the negatives were potentially fatal flaws and should have been seriously evaluated.

Beginning the Search

The work you did in chapters 2 and 5 to narrow your focus to a certain type of business will now help you explore various industries and businesses.

If you are simply curious about what is for sale, start by searching the Internet for "businesses for sale." Many business brokers have multiple listing services (MLS) websites, just like realty companies do for listing homes for sale. A quick Google search found more than 250,000 websites to explore. Some websites have listings by location, others by business type.

Once you decide you are serious about buying a business, consider working with a business broker who is a Certified Business Intermediary (CBI). This is a great option for a first-time business buyer. There are many reasons to seek out a CBI rather than a generic business broker. The primary reason, however, is because less than 5% of brokers hold the CBI designation (which requires a minimum of three years of experience, and seventy hours of curriculum with rigorous testing). Consequently, those brokers without CBI designations may be much less experienced and knowledgeable. In fact, there is no established training required to become a business broker, and some of them really have no clue what they are doing. This could be very bad for you. There certainly are brilliant, honest, and knowledgeable business brokers who aren't CBIs, but you would need to spend more time getting references and verifying the scope of their expertise if you go this route.

For the sake of expediency, however, I'll use the generic term *broker* during the rest of this discussion on business brokers. I assume you will conduct thorough background checks on your choice of a broker.

Keep in mind that business brokers are like Realtors; some work with buyers to find a house and others work with sellers to find buyers.

In our situation, the broker's role is to help you find businesses that are of interest and are well matched to you. He or she will also work through the due diligence with you and help negotiate the purchase terms and conditions. Because of their experience, they will identify things that don't sound or look right during the due diligence process. And they'll recognize potential red flags that you are likely to miss.

Brokers get paid when you buy a business. And, like a Realtor, a broker could be in a position to represent both the buyer and the seller, which dramatically increases the broker's incentive to close the deal. So just make sure you always know the broker's potential financial gain on any business he or she recommends you purchase.

If the business you are interested in is already for sale, then the seller will pay the broker's fees, and this is already included in the purchase price. As you look into each business opportunity, make sure you know how the broker will be paid because it may vary. Some specialty broker practices only represent buyers; others represent only sellers. Unfortunately for many people purchasing a Plan B business, specialty business brokers are typically found only with businesses starting at the fifty-million-dollar price level and higher.

However, since you are not likely looking at a fifty-million-dollar business, you will work with someone who has represented both sellers and buyers in the past. Just keep confirming how that broker will be paid for each business opportunity he or she presents to you. There is nothing wrong with a broker presenting the business opportunities that provide the highest incentives—as long as you know about it. One of those opportunities may even be the best choice for you.

If you end up working with a business broker who legally represents the seller, remember that the broker will use everything you have said or anything they know about you to get a higher price for the seller. Also, they are legally prohibited from providing you any advice about the purchase. This is why you should have your own broker to guide you through the process.

Protecting the Seller's Information and Proving Your Financial Resources

During your due diligence on a specific business, you will receive confidential and intimate details: customers, suppliers, employees, business performance, and possibly even some trade secrets. Not surprisingly, you will be required to sign a Non-Disclosure and Confidentiality Agreement as soon as you make the first call to the seller's business broker. This protects the seller so you don't share those details with anyone else. One of the first things the selling broker will do is to find out if you are a competitor. In some cases, competitors make good buyers. For example, if you own a hardware store in a neighboring community, you are a competitor but probably not one that could hurt the business. So the seller may approve you. This type of competitor is different than one who is a block away; the seller may understandably not want that buyer to have access to confidential business details.

You will also be required to provide personal financial data to ensure you have the financial resources to buy the business. You don't need to disclose your entire wealth—only enough to prove you can afford the down payment. Your bank can provide a letter of credit stating this. Other financial data that could be used are personal net worth statements that include cash in the bank, stocks, and other investments and income sources. Some brokers may ask you to provide a personal financial statement (signed and dated), copies of personal income tax returns (usually three years' worth), and a credit report. The specific requirements will vary by seller.

Conducting Your Due Diligence

The process of buying a business will require you to read and understand a lot of detailed information in order to complete your own evaluation and analysis as part of your due diligence. Even if you work with a broker, you need to personally understand the business information described next. In the end, the final decision to buy a company will be yours, and you want to make the smartest decision you can.

You need to review two sets of information. The first is the *Business Listing Information,* which offers a short and crisp description of the business. The second set is the *Selling Memorandum,* which provides more detailed and specific information on the key elements of the business.[4]

1. The *Business Listing Information* contains overview information. Use it to quickly decide to either eliminate the business from further consideration or determine if you want additional information. Similar to the MLS real estate listings to buy a house, the Business Listing Information will contain industry data, a business description, the general geographical location (such as northern Georgia), the selling price, gross revenues, and the cash flow. It will also list any inventory, equipment, leases, and real estate that may be part of the purchase. Look for an executive summary about the business, and information on how to contact the listing broker or agent.

If you decide you are interested, you will request the second set of information, the *Selling Memorandum.*

2. A *Selling Memorandum* is also called a *Confidential Business Summary* or a *Confidential Business Review.* A good one must do two (often conflicting) tasks: present completely factual information and create interest, excitement, and a compelling reason to buy now. Advertisers do the same thing when they create a sense of urgency or imply a scarcity. The components of a Selling Memorandum should include:

- *Executive summary:* The summary will concisely describe the key elements of the business in a way that is appealing to the buyer.
- *Company:* This section provides background information on the company, owners, and management staff.
- *Offer:* The offer lists what is for sale (assets, stock, or real estate), the asking price, and the terms of the sale. Increasingly, sellers have to carry part of the loan (called *holding paper*) because it's harder to borrow money these days due to the stricter loan requirements. The offer includes factors that increase the value of the business, such as exclusive contracts, patents, or competitive advantages.
- *Products/services:* This section describes competitors' products and services and how the company competes effectively with them. It is designed to demonstrate knowledge of the competitive strengths and weaknesses of the business and to reduce the buyer's risk of the unknown.
- *Profitability:* The company's major products or services will each have a profitability report. If the profits come from a variety of products or services, the business will be worth more than if most of the profits come from just one area. Having only one profitable offering makes the company vulnerable to substitutions by competitors.
- *Industry:* This section outlines the industry status, trends, and financial standards. A business will have a higher value if an industry is growing and a company's market share is expanding.
- *Customers:* This section will identify if most of the company's sales come from just a few cus-

tomers or from a larger number of customers. The profitability levels for the key customers should be included here as well.

- *Competitors:* This section explains the company's market share and identifies its competitors. It explains how competitors interact with each other. The intensity of the competition—such as fierce, moderate, or passive—should be rated and listed in this section.

- *Marketing plan:* This is an inside look at the company's marketing activities, including overall strategy, pricing policy, and the methods of selling, advertising, and promotions. Sales are the lifeblood of the business, so spend time understanding the customers and the sales cycle and process.

- *Strengths, weaknesses, opportunities, and threats (SWOT):* The SWOT analysis identifies the company's important risks, assumptions, and problems. It also describes actions or strategies that could be used to overcome these potential problems.

- *Geography:* This section describes the city and state as a potential place to live. This information may be important to out-of-state buyers.

- *Production/operating plan:* The plan describes the production method and/or delivery of services.

- *Financials:* This is critical, and it is where you will do 80%-90% of the work involved in buying a business.

It's important to know that prior to selling a business, most sellers report as little profits as possible to keep taxes low. Thus, they typically recast (for potential buyers) the financial statements to prove the maximum earning power of the business. The higher the earnings and cash flow, the more the buyer will typically pay. Here is an example of a financial recast: $100,000 cash flow is shown; however, the company paid taxes on only $65,000 of profit. So where is the other $35,000? The owner's compensation might have been $25,000, and the remaining $10,000 was paid to the bank in interest for debt the company holds (the company wouldn't typically pay taxes on this $35,000). So the recast statement more accurately shows $65,000 in profit, plus $25,000 in owner compensation, plus $10,000 in interest.

You should also identify other discretionary spending by the seller. For example, a car listed as a company car has to be proven as such. The seller might say he uses the vehicle to make deliveries, and that's why it's a legitimate expense. Some owners will write off vacations as a business expense which you will, of course, ask him to prove. In the recast, you will find the details of what is business versus personal expenses.

These two sets of information—the Business Listing Information and the Selling Memorandum—are the biggest part of your due diligence. Your business broker should be doing most of the work on the profit and loss statements, the tax review, and the other financial analyses.

Lou Vescio has more due diligence advice to share with you:

"You need to analyze the industry trends. In most industries, sales are currently down from 2006 to 2008 levels. To find out if the industry has stopped bleeding, look at the sales for the last two to three years. If they are flat, then the bleeding has stopped. If sales went up, that is great. If the industry sales are still dropping, then the bleeding has not stopped and you will want to wait until it levels off. Otherwise you may be paying too much for a business or, in the worst case, buying one that won't survive.

"Let's use a window and door business I have been working with recently as an example. In 2005 and 2006, the company had between $1.5 and $2.0 million in sales. In 2007, sales were $1 million. In 2008, they were $750,000. In 2009, sales tumbled to $500,000 and remained there in 2010. So it looks like sales leveled off in 2010 and aren't continuing to drop. The industry trends show the same pattern, so that is another positive.

"You also need to look at sales month by month for the last three to four years, to see how cyclical they are. For example, many restaurants and retail stores in Florida make most of their sales from November to May. If you buy the business in June, you will need cash to keep it going until sales pick up again in November. Retail stores across the United States typically make 95% of their profits in November and December, which means you need to have enough cash to keep the business going for the other ten months. (Black Friday, the day after Thanksgiving in the United States, is the first day of the year most retail businesses are profitable, i.e., they're in the black.)

"Understanding the accounts receivable is also critical. Let's use the example of a restoration business that cleans up a house or office building after a flood. The payment does not come from the owner; it comes from the insurance company. Most insurance companies make it a practice to delay payments for three to four months, but the owner must pay for the supplies and the labor as they are used. In such cases, the owner may need a substantial line of credit to use for operating capital to carry the business until insurance checks start coming in.

"Assets are another key piece of your due diligence. I'm working with a liquor store right now that has an asking price of $600,000, with assets of $200,000 of inventory, which won't spoil or expire very quickly, if at all. The liquor license, worth $150,000, is another asset. So out of the $600,000 asking price, $350,000 of it are valuable and relatively liquid (not meant to be a pun) assets that significantly reduce the risk of the acquisition.

"You should also know the industry's number of inventory turns (how many times the inventory is sold in a year). If the sales price is $500,000 and the industry turns the inventory only two times a year, make sure you know how much of the purchase price is in inventory. Electronics and women's clothing become dated relatively quickly, and you may not be able to sell them. If there is between $200,000 and $300,000 in inventory that will expire or become outdated, the sales price may be too high.

"Before investing a great deal of your money in a business, I recommend you have the business appraised by a competent business appraiser. If you apply for an SBA loan, the lending bank will hire such an appraiser before making the loan."

After you complete all of your due diligence, if you are still interested in buying the business, then the next step is to meet the seller.

Meeting with the Seller

Meeting with the seller or sellers is the last 10%-20% of the buying process.

The seller is going to do all he can to make the business look attractive. Your job is to look behind the curtain and under the rug to see what really takes place. You have done most of the work already. Now, however, you'll want to enlist experts, such as a business broker, a banker, and/or an accountant specializing in small business, to help you come up with the right questions to ask. Fundamental questions include why the owners are selling, how they spend their day-to-day time running the business, what type of transition they are thinking about, and how they arrived at their asking price. You definitely want your team in the meeting with you because most sellers only answer questions they're specifically asked.

As part of your evaluation, walk around and inspect the facilities, and see which furniture, fixtures, and equipment come with the business. Take pictures to ensure that what you see stays with the business and that there are no last-minute swaps.

After you and your team finish your due diligence on the business by analyzing the business and industry trends, business profitability, and competitors, it's time to decide if you remain interested in buying the business.

If so, the offer comes next.

Making the Offer

There are two ways to make an offer: with a *Letter of Intent* (LOI) or with an *Offer to Purchase* (also called a *Contract with Contingencies*). Either one requires earnest money from you.

A *Letter of Intent* is not binding, but it will tie up the business for 2-3 months so no other offers can be received or considered. The LOI gives you time to complete the rest of your due diligence, especially the requirements of the sellers to prove to you that what they have claimed is accurate. Bankers are very good at helping with this; they typically don't believe what anyone claims. And if the business qualifies for an SBA loan, you'll have even more due diligence as part of the process.

An *Offer to Purchase,* on the other hand, becomes legally binding once all of the contingencies have been met. Examples of contingencies could include you receiving approval for a loan, confirming when the lease can be signed over to you, and verifying the length of time the seller will remain with the business during a transition period. If it is a franchise, you will need approval from the franchise corporation to purchase the individual franchise.

Your experts should work with you here. The negotiation process typically includes reaching an agreement on the terms and conditions that both you and the seller want, so be sure your attorney reviews it. Your continued due diligence will verify all information in the documents, validate the accuracy of financial data, review equipment leases, get facility and equipment inspections, get approvals for any special license or permit, check on any liens that the business and the seller have, and get your loan approved.

And just like buying a house, after everything has been reviewed and approved, you will finalize the sale, exchange the documents and the money, and receive the keys to your Plan B business.

At this point, congratulations are in order!

Wrap Up

We have walked through the good and bad news about buying a business, as well as the advantages and disadvantages. You learned that buying an existing business can potentially have a higher success rate than starting one. You were introduced to the concept of business brokers, and how to evaluate and use them. We applied the Six Key Ingredients from chapter 6 to Paul's tanning salon business and analyzed those results, and did the same with the results of the Real Deal Checklist we started using in chapter 7. You now know that 80%-90% of your efforts need to focus on analyzing the business' financial data. You also now know the specific steps involved in buying a business.

In the next chapter, we will explore the world of franchising. It is another way to buy a business, one that offers turnkey solutions that have been duplicated more than once.

You will also learn the good and bad news about buying a franchise and the advantages and disadvantages. We will cover the restrictions and controls franchisors typically impose on franchisees, and the four types of franchise models. We also apply the Six Key Ingredients to a variety of franchises and then study those results. We will discuss how to find franchisors and what to look for in one. Then we will explore how to find, evaluate, and use franchise brokers and advisors. The section on the government-mandated Franchise Disclosure Document (FDD) explains the purpose of an FDD: to provide you with detailed information about a specific franchise. And, just like when buying a business, most of your due diligence will be analyzing the company's financial information.

Turn the page to continue on your journey as we explore the world of franchises...

Notes

1   Lou Vescio
      Certified Business Intermediary (CBI)
      Coastal Business Intermediaries, Inc., Melbourne, FL
      www.agencybrokerageconsultants.com

2   The Formula for Return on Investment (ROI) is:
      ROI = Gain from Investment + Cost of Investment = Cost of Investment

3   The General Equation for Return on Invested Capital (ROIC) is: ROIC = Net Income – Dividends/Total Capital

4   Lou Vescio
      Certified Business Intermediary (CBI)
      Coastal Business Intermediaries, Inc., Melbourne, FL
      www.agencybrokerageconsultants.com

CHAPTER 9

The Real Deal about Buying a Franchise

FRANCHISING CAN BE described as *a business in a box,* which means you buy a business that already has systems in place for every aspect of running it, including the products and services, marketing and sales, operations, accounting, hiring and training employees, customer service, and technology systems.

It is similar to the process of buying a business that we looked at in chapter 8, except the business has been duplicated more than once. A good franchise will automatically give you local and/or national branding with proven products and services. In theory, you have a blueprint for success, and the franchisor will train you on how to use it.

Franchises are big business. It is estimated that more than 700,000 franchise options are available. Think about any of your areas of interest and you can probably find a franchise that matches it. Examples of service franchises include home repair and remodeling, food catering, and maintenance and cleaning services. Business-support (i.e., B2B) franchise examples are accounting, mail processing, advertising services, package wrapping and shipping, staffing and temporary help services, and printing and copying. Consumer-needs franchise examples include hair salons, massage centers, pet care, and fitness centers. Most product-based franchises sell some type of food—such as sandwiches, beverages, and ice cream—from a storefront, vending machine, or a van.

Franchising is the third in the four ways to create a Plan B. As with the two previous chapters on starting or buying a business, what you have learned about yourself in chapters 2 and 5 will help you determine if this is good match. For example, running a franchise might be great if you like having an established way to do business—if routine is important to you because it brings order, predictability, and security to your work life. On the other hand, if you like doing new things every day, owning a franchise is probably not the best option because the franchisor has determined exactly how you will operate the business, and there may not be an opportunity to use your creativity.

By using the tools in this book and making a commitment to do your due diligence, you will greatly increase your chances of personal and financial success if you choose buying a franchise for your Plan B.

Let's define the terms we will use in this chapter:

> A franchise has three key components: use of a trademark, payment of a franchise and royalty fees, and ongoing support.
>
> —ED TEIXEIRA, FRANCHISE KNOW HOW, LLC; AUTHOR, *HOW TO BUY A FRANCHISE*[1]

- *Franchisor.* The *franchisor* sells a business concept for a one-time fee, and collects ongoing royalties that are typically a percentage of gross sales.
- *Franchisee.* The person who buys the franchise is the *franchisee* and can use the franchisor's trade name and systems.

- *Franchise.* The contract combining the two is the *franchise,* although the term is also used to describe the business the franchisee is running.
- *Franchise broker.* The *franchise broker* is like a matchmaker between the franchisor and the franchisee. They may have their own business and may represent up to two hundred different franchisors, or they may work for only one. Like car sales, brokers get paid on commission and only if the deal closes.
- *Franchise advisor.* The *franchise advisor* is paid a flat fee to act as a guide and coach through the buying process. You are buying their experience and expertise to help you find the right franchise model for you.
- *Franchise consultant.* A *franchise consultant* works with business owners who want to franchise their business.
- *Franchise Disclosure Document (FDD).* The *FDD* is the federally mandated document franchisors are required to provide with detailed information in twenty-three areas of their operations.

As always in this *real deal guide,* I will give you both the good and the bad news about franchises.

The *good news* about the franchise option for your Plan B is that the hard parts of making a business successful have already been figured out and duplicated multiple times. The company name and its branding are more widely known, making it easier for you to attract customers and employees. As a result, this option may be safer than starting your own business.

The *bad news* is that, just like any other business, franchise companies can fail, and you can too. Another thing to remember is that you will typically be doing

> "The reason most individual franchise units fail today is not because they bought the wrong franchise. It is because of the personality of the owners. They don't follow the proven model. Franchises require compliance."
>
> —PETER CARLSON, ENTREPRENEUR, FRANCHISE BROKER[2]

the same work day after day, month after month. So if you get bored easily, either this is not the business model for you or you will want a partner who loves working this way (and thus freeing you up to oversee other aspects of the business). You will also have to give up some of your independence and do things the way the franchisor directs you to, but that is not much different than having a job, and you already know how to do that, don't you?

Sometimes franchises are described as a way to buy yourself a job, because the franchisee can't be fired like an employee can. The franchise could only be lost if the franchisee does not live up to the standards or use the systems established in the contract. (More on those circumstances later in this chapter.)

Below is a conversation I had with two thirty-something men after I gave a speech on Plan B to a large group. This conversation provides two situations with quite different outcomes, although both are fast-food franchises. The first man, Andy, is a believer in franchises. His father-in-law had bought a fast-food franchise and recruited the family to help him run it.

> "Many of us already had other jobs so it was a matter of coordinating schedules and days. My full-time job was on second shift, so I opened the store every morning and my father-in-law came in after his regular job was over and stayed until we closed at 11:00 p.m.

> "It was eighteen months of working seven days a week to get it launched. Three years later, he sold it for a profit of $300,000—a pretty good one for just three years."

"There are no valid statistics supporting the success rate of franchises. In 2005, the International Franchise Association issued a memorandum to its members acknowledging the invalidity of statistics they had published showing high success rates. They requested the statistics be removed from websites; few have."

—SEAN KELLY, PRESIDENT, IDEA-FARM; PUBLISHER, FRANCHISEMARKETING. COM[3]

The second man, Greg, chimed in to share with us a friend's franchising experience.

> "Richard was getting laid off again, the third time in four years. His nerves were shot and the job market was bleak. It was time for a Plan B, so he decided to buy himself a job. He attended several seminars on franchises and wanted to buy a food franchise. Since he could not get financing, he cashed out his 401(k) and set up his sandwich shop near a college campus.
>
> "Now, two years later, he is still working 60–80 hours a week because employee turnover is so high. Apparently, no one wants to work very hard. He is sick of making sandwiches every single day. He is exhausted and can't take the time off for a vacation. He has tried to find a buyer so he can at least recover his initial investment, but the people who are interested can't get financing and want him to underwrite the deal. If he had only known…"

…or done a bit more due diligence, I thought.

In the first situation, Andy's father-in-law bought a national franchise in a great location. With help from his family and by working hard, he sold it for a nice profit, which was his exit strategy. Everyone kept their full-time jobs and figured out how to build their franchise part-time. It worked very well for him.

Richard, on the other hand, was clearly buying himself a job. After being laid off as an employee so many times, he knew that franchisees could not be fired. It may still be a good Plan B for Richard if he can

---

FRANCHISE CATEGORY SIZE

Fast-food restaurants—categorized as limited-service restaurants by the US Census Bureau—has 125,898 establishments and topped the list of all franchise operations, followed by 33,391 gas stations with convenience stores, and 30,130 full-service restaurants.

FRANCHISE SALES

New-car dealers led sales for franchise businesses with $687.7 billion, followed by $131.1 billion from gas stations with convenience stores, and $112.0 billion from fast-food restaurants.

—2007 ECONOMIC CENSUS DATA REPORT, AS QUOTED IN THE FRANCHISE BUYER'S MANUAL, ED TEIXEIRA[5]

reduce his employee turnover and attract a good partner to buy in to part of the business and help him with the work.

Should you buy yourself a job? The answer is...maybe.

"However, be very careful," says John Lucht, author of *Rites of Passage at $100,000 to $1 Million+*. John is the founder and owner of RiteSite.com, a career transition company for corporate executives.[4] He has worked for decades to help executives figure out what to do next as they were bought out, laid off, or fired from their jobs. He helped some clients start a company; others he helped evaluate options to buy a business. Here is what he told one client who asked him about buying a franchise:

> "The excitement of being your own boss; ditching those mindless meetings; the dream that you can take control of your life—these can be very seductive. Certainly the endless rounds of submitting résumés, getting the rare interview, and trying to ignore a sneaking suspicion that age discrimination is alive and well can make buying yourself a job look like your best option. And it may well be. But there are some key explorations and due diligence to complete before risking your life savings."

John has two hard-and-fast rules for would-be franchisees who face persuasive franchise sales pitches. The rules make a lot of sense, and they complement the work you did in chapters 2 and 5.

- If it is something you would *not* have looked at if you had a good job, then *don't* look at it now. If, when you think about it, you gut tightens or you are embarrassed to tell others, then it is probably not for you.

- Work at a unit for at least one week without anyone knowing your purchasing intent. Drive as far as you have to, even stay in a motel. Get yourself hired at a low-level job and stand behind the counter or desk of the business you are ready to risk your life savings on.

As with each of the Plan B options, you will need to allow plenty of time to conduct your own due diligence before deciding to buy a franchise.

Below are several additional questions to ask yourself. They complement the questions you answered in chapter 2.

- What is the type of technical experience, special training, or education that is needed? Do I already have it? Examples: tax preparation, interior design, or car repair skills.
- How will I gain a complete understanding of the business? Examples: work as an employee for the franchise and learn all that I can, or find a successful franchisee in the same or a similar chain to mentor me.
- What hours and what level of personal commitment are needed to run the business? Am I ready and willing to do what is demanded?

Franchising 101

Remember, a franchisor was once a business start-up that was successful. The owner typically opened a second location and then maybe a third. At some point, the owner wanted to grow the brand's name and profitability but

EVEN BIG-NAME FRANCHISES CAN RUN INTO PROBLEMS

Quiznos Subs was sued by franchisees claiming price gouging because they were required to buy overpriced supplies from the corporation. The lawsuit was settled in 2009.

—WALL STREET JOURNAL (WSJ), JULY 21, 2011

Curves' 2010 Franchise Disclosure Document (FDD) disclosed 28 civil actions in the Litigation section. One suit alleged such things as breach of contract, fraudulent inducement, and negligent misrepresentation.

—UNHAPPY FRANCHISEE.COM[6]

did not want to be involved in the day-to-day operations, so he or she sold the business concept to others. To do this, the original business owner simply had to develop a way to duplicate the successful start-up's systems for operations, marketing, and accounting.

But purchasing a franchise is like every other investment: There's no guarantee of success. Some franchises have a consistent record of success, while others have a high failure rate.

According to recent estimates, there are more than 4,000 franchise business concepts available in 75 different industry categories[7] that, combined, create 700,000 franchise establishments[8] for sale. Also, there are more than 400 US-based franchise systems that operate internationally.[9]

Just a few of the industries in which franchise opportunities abound include advertising/direct mail, construction, dating services, home inspection, security systems, maid services, computer services, cleaners, lawn-care services, real estate, hotels and motels, and travel agencies. Since the list can be overwhelming, aren't you glad you have already done so much work to discover your interests and preferred work lifestyle?

The US Census Bureau reports that one out of every ten businesses is a franchised business. The franchise sector has annual sales estimated at over $1.3 trillion.[10] The initial cost of a franchise can range from $30,000 to over $2 million, but it's hard to buy a good franchise for less than $50,000, reports Lou Vescio of Coastal Business Intermediaries, Inc.

Don't equate the level of investment in a franchise to its profitability. A $500,000 investment may not even create an annual profit over $100,000. However, there are franchises costing from $50,000 to $100,000 that you can build into a six-figure business by picking the right one, having it in the right community and location (if it is a storefront), and working very hard.

In keeping with the *real deal* promise to provide you with a balanced picture of each Plan B option, let's cover the advantages and disadvantages of franchising.

Franchises Have Many Advantages

A franchise could be a good choice for your Plan B because it has unique advantages that the other Plan B options don't.

- **Instant name recognition and branding.** The McDonald's arches are instantly recognized around the world. This level of recognition can be a great savings in the cost of acquiring customers.
- **Turnkey operations with established operations, marketing, and accounting models.** The franchise system is a proven model for operating a business usually at a profit. If you are weak in certain areas of operating a business, the franchisor has already figured it out for you.
- **Training and support systems.** Small business owners often have very little support and lack a team with business expertise. Franchise organizations have created the systems you will need for yourself and your employees to be trained properly. Then, if you get stuck, a problem-solving team is theoretically there for you.
- **Easier recruiting.** Finding good employees is a critical success factor for all business owners. With your

"Franchises can be lower risk [than other business ventures], if the candidate selects the right franchise business for them, has enough of a financial cushion to get him or her through the start-up phase, and uses a franchise lawyer to help digest the FDD and the contract.

But even with perfect circumstances, people can fail in a franchise business, just like they can get fired from a perfect job."

—JOEL LIBAVA,
FRANCHISE ADVISOR,
FRANCHISE SELECTION SPECIALISTS,
INC.[11]

franchise's recognized name, you will automatically be more attractive to applicants than an unfamiliar business would. Two graduate students looking for jobs both told me that they were focusing their search on nationally known companies. They named the franchises with which they were interviewing and felt the management would automatically be good and the wages would be better than those of a local company.

- **Lower inventory prices.** The buying power of a franchise group allows for lower costs when purchasing inventory and equipment.

- **Higher success rates, at times.** Franchises have a proven model of success, although some are more successful and profitable than others. Therefore, you will want to know which franchises outperform the others. You can do your own homework or use the knowledgeable assistance of a franchise broker.

- **Government regulations.** The Federal Trade Commission (FTC) requires a franchisor to provide full disclosure before a potential franchisee purchases the business. This is communicated through a Franchise Disclosure Document (FDD). A few of the categories that are required to be disclosed are the directors' and principal officers' business background for at least the last five years, the financials of the organization, litigation (including any pending lawsuits, lawsuits involving the franchise relationship, prior lawsuits, current government injunctive or restrictive actions and arbitrations). Every FDD should also include lists of both the current franchisees and those who have left in the last twelve months; you will use these lists to conduct your due diligence. (More information on the FDD appears later in this chapter.)

Franchises Also Have Disadvantages

As with all of the Plan B options, franchises have some drawbacks you should know about.

- **Expensive to open and operate.** Once past the initial purchase or transfer fee, royalties are paid monthly to the franchisor based on your gross sales. Royalties typically range from 4% to 12%, with the average being 6%. With a 6% royalty, for example, you pay the franchisor six cents on every sales dollar you earn.

> "Be careful of high-flying franchises. If they grow too quickly, they may not be able to deliver long term. What is hot today may fall flat tomorrow."
>
> —ED TEIXEIRA, FRANCHISE KNOW HOW, LLC; AUTHOR, *HOW TO BUY A FRANCHISE*[12]

There are also local and national advertising fees to be paid weekly or monthly. In some cases, this fee is not connected to your gross sales volume; in others, it is 1%-2% of sales. You have neither control nor input on how this money is spent on advertising.

You are also expected to have your own cash resources for a down payment on the business. Few franchisors offer financing, but many are able to refer you to financial lenders who do. Just as you need cash reserves to cover living expenses for a length of time like the first two Plan B options, you will need to determine your cash flow and profitability here too.

- **Not all franchises are good, reputable, or profitable.** This is where you want to spend your research time because, after all, you are buying a franchise to make money. Work with an accountant who is an expert in franchising so you can calculate your break-even point (how long until you have recovered your investment and are making a profit.) Franchisors provide to you the costs and expense numbers in the FDD, but most do not provide the sales figures

> "Franchisors already have a specific marketing plan in place. They will have preset advertising templates for you to use, and you cannot use your own without their permission."
>
> —Joel Libava, franchise advisor, Franchise Selection Specialists, Inc.[13]

by franchise units. By talking with franchisees and getting their earnings numbers, you can run a *pro forma* statement and determine the profitability. See why you need an accountant?

Another point is to verify a franchisor's financial success comes from the sales of their products and services and not primarily from selling franchises. For example, a once-darling of the coffee-shop-franchise industry was expanding from Canada into the northeastern United States, yet their record earnings came from selling franchises and not their coffee. As a result, it appeared to perspective franchisees that the brand was profitable, but in reality the record profits at that time were coming from selling franchises and not from royalties based on store sales. It does not mean that the franchise will not be profitable via royalties—it's simply important to understand where the money is coming from.

- **Limited expansion capability.** If you want to expand, your franchisor will typically require you to buy another franchise. If it is a storefront, you will buy rights to another location. If it is a service company, you will buy a new territory.

- **Significant risk.** Franchises can fail too. You may have to deal with broken promises if the franchisor cannot fulfill its commitments or provide the support you need. One specialty-wine-store franchisee found out his franchisor had gone out of business when an employee from their headquarters applied for a job with him.

- **Comply with their rules.** The franchisor has developed, tested, and implemented a specific way to run the business. If you are someone who likes to make most decisions on your own or you like to do things your way, a franchise will not be right for you. As a franchise owner, you must comply with the various controls and procedures established by the franchisor. (More specific information in the section below covers controls and restrictions.)

Franchise Controls and Restrictions

To ensure uniformity, franchisors usually control how franchisees conduct business. This is a good news–bad news aspect of the franchise industry. While these controls may hamper your ability to use your own business judgment, they can also ensure your franchise keeps it value.

Here are some of the rules you can expect:

- **Site approval.** The location is always critical and therefore the franchisor reserves the right to preapprove sites. The reviews and approvals are designed to maximize your customer traffic and success. Your preferred spot may not be approved for such reasons as the franchisor's concerns about zoning, parking, traffic flow, competition, or government utilities. This control can prevent you from choosing a bad location that could lead to a business failure.

- **Design or appearance standards.** By ensuriing that all franchises have a standard look, the company reinforces the brand and name recognition you, as a franchisee, are buying. Signage and uniforms are common examples. For example, UPS has a specific brown color that is used to brand its trucks

3 MOST COMMON FRANCHISE-SELECTION MISTAKES

1. A bad fit between the franchisee's interests and the product or service of the franchise.

2. It is beyond the financial means of the franchisee. (Be sure you have three to six months' working capital.)

3. The franchisee is overanxious and jumps into the deal without clearly understanding the disclosure documents, without seeking legal advice of attorneys with experience in franchising, and without using written documents to verify verbal claims of the franchisor.

—ED TEIXEIRA, FRANCHISE KNOW HOW, LLC; AUTHOR, HOW TO BUY A FRANCHISE[12]

and stores. Franchisees do not have the option to add splashes of other colors.

- **Restrictions on goods and services you sell.** The franchisor has established the business offerings to ensure your customers know what they can expect when they come to you. Selling a completely different product or service, such as a massage business that starts selling luggage, would create customer confusion.

These restrictions also prevent any sales from being diverted away from the franchisor's core offerings. For example, a clothing store franchisee adds a third-party line of jewelry that competes with the franchisor's offering. When a customer buys the new jewelry product instead of something else in the store, the franchisor loses the royalty and profit.

- **Restrictions on method of operation.** The franchisor will spell out the specific hours, signs, employee uniforms, and advertisements you will have. There will be predetermined accounting or bookkeeping procedures. Goods or services will sell at specific prices. Discounts are restricted, and you'll be required to buy supplies from approved suppliers regardless of lower prices elsewhere. This prevents you from supporting local businesses that you might otherwise prefer to buy from.

- **Restrictions on sales area.** You will be required to limit your business to a specific geographic or industry territory, your website is predesigned, and what you can offer on your website has already been determined. The franchisor may also compete directly with you by offering the same products and services via the Internet. For example, if you buy a computer franchise, the franchisor may offer an option for customers to buy their computer online at a discounted price—bypassing you.

- **Terminations and renewals.** Each franchisor has restrictions stated in the contract with a franchisee. If you breach the contract, you can lose your franchise and investment. The contract terms are typically ten years, but your right to renew is not automatic or guaranteed. You may have to meet a minimum monthly sales volume, too, in addition to other things we've discussed.

  But to actually lose your franchise, you would typically have to be a really bad franchisee. For example, if you are an oil-changing business and don't recycle the used oil properly, or if you don't pay the fees and royalties you owe the franchisor, you could lose your franchise and your franchise investment fee.

  Franchisors want you to be successful and renew the contract because that is how they make money. Your contract spells out exactly what is expected and what would trigger a problem with your ability to renew.

Each franchise will spell out all of its controls and restrictions. The FDD also has a section with franchisor and franchisee obligations. The intent is to ensure the brand remains consistent and therefore strong and valuable. Consumers choose your products and services because they trust the brand and expect consistent quality, which is what the franchisor should be providing to you, too.

Four Franchise Models

There are four types of franchise combinations, starting with a single franchise unit.[15] From there, the options increase based on the number of units, the rights, and the investment levels.

The first model is buying a single franchise. The second, often called a multi-unit, is when the franchisee buys more than one unit. The third type is a development franchise with exclusive territory rights, and the requirement to open and sell a number of units in a specific timeframe. The fourth and final model is a master or regional developer who acts in a business development role with exclusive franchise rights in a geographic area. Here is more information on each of them.

- **Single Franchise.** This is the first level and the most common form of franchise participation. The franchisee is awarded the exclusive rights to operate a single-unit franchise in a specified geographic area. This is usually a hands-on business. Some franchisors will not sell a new store to someone who has not managed one successfully before. That means if you want that specific franchise, you will have to buy one from an existing owner. (There is more information on how to buy an existing franchise later in the chapter.)

- **Multi-unit Franchise.** The franchisee owns and operates more than one franchise unit in different locations or areas. The owner is usually less involved with each unit but manages the overall operations. Some franchisors will not let you buy just one unit; they require you to buy two.

- **Area-Development Franchising.** The franchisee will own exclusive rights to a territory and will agree to a development schedule for the number of units they must open, sell, and operate. This allows the franchisor to have more "feet on the street" promoting and selling the franchisor's products and services and, eventually, the franchise itself. In this situation, franchisors normally reduce significantly their franchise fees and possibly even the ongoing royalties owed. For example, Great Clips offers a reduction in fee with area development agreements.

- **Master Franchising.** Also called a master or regional developer, this franchising model has exclusive rights granted in a geographic area, just as the area-development model does. However, in the master franchising model, the master developer acts as the business development partner for the franchise company in its specific territory or region, i.e., a state, a county, or a metropolitan area. The master franchisee is expected to open and sell single-unit and multiunit franchises. They recruit franchisees and work closely with them to help them make the right site selections, open their franchises, and become successful. The master developer profits from the work by retaining a significant portion of the franchise fee, as well as ongoing royalties from the franchisees within that geographical area. This allows the master franchisor to create wealth because of the income from the fees and royalties. These master developers are highly motivated to make sure you succeed.

If you're a franchise newbie, I recommend sticking to the simplest franchise model, which is a single franchise. Then, as you master the work, you can grow the business by purchasing more units. This is the most common model for a first-time franchisee.

After that, franchisees can shift to the area-development franchise model, which requires significantly more knowledge, skills, and experience in franchise development because the job is now to build, open, and sell franchise units. And just like a home-building contractor, area-development franchisees have the geographic area locked in.

The master or regional developer does similar work, but in this model, they also serve as business development partners and collect fees and royalties for their efforts. Understandably, this requires extensive knowledge in business and franchising, so the beginning franchisee does not start here.

Selecting a Franchise

There are numerous books, publications, and websites available to help you better understand the franchising world and specific franchisors. For example, the Federal Trade Commission (www.ftc.gov) has a valuable free publication entitled *Consumer Guide to Buying a Franchise.* The International Franchise Association has a *Franchise Opportunities Guide* with a list of more than seventy-five businesses selling franchises. You can purchase the guide at the association's online bookstore (www.franchise.org). This association supports the franchisors. On the other hand, the American Association of Franchisees and Dealers (AAFD) represent franchisees and independent dealers (www.aafd.org). They can help you find other franchise owners in your area with the same brand.

Buying a franchise is like buying any other business: the most successful options have the Six Key Ingredients from chapter 6, and they scored high on the Real Deal Checklist from chapter 7. Later we will apply the Six Key Ingredients and the Real Deal Checklist to various franchises to give you several more examples of how to use them yourself.

However, before working through them, here are a few more questions to consider that complement the work you have done in chapters 2 and 5 that helped you decide what *you* need from your Plan B.

- Does my experience help me in this industry? If you have no background in the industry, it may take you longer to build your business.
- Can I be trained and learn what I need to run the franchise? Can I learn what I don't know from the franchisor or from other sources? You will need to learn new skills, and it will take time.
- Will I accept the controls, guidance, and direction that the franchisor will impose? You must read and understand the manuals developed for the business and then follow them exactly.
- How do I personally feel about the company's image, products, and services? You want a good feeling about your business, because you will be working in it for years, even decades.
- Am I willing to work the hours and days required for the franchise? Keep in mind that franchise contracts are typically ten years. Be sure this is a good fit, so you wake up happy to go to work every day.
- How much money do I need to have to buy a franchise? Make sure you are realistic about the initial investment and the ongoing cost of running the

> "If you are not sales oriented, don't buy a business to business (B2B) franchise that requires you to sell to businesses. You will be miserable each day as you make sales calls."
>
> —Ed Teixeira, Franchise Know How, LLC; author, *How to Buy a Franchise* [12]

business. Don't overextend yourself if you find a dazzling opportunity you can't resist.

Let's now apply the Six Key Ingredients to see how they can help evaluate the franchises that interest you.

Six Key Ingredients for Evaluating a Franchise

The Six Key Ingredients are applied to a variety of offerings so you can learn how to apply them to yours.

1. **Market trends in your favor.** One example of a growing market trend is the dramatic increase in diabetes in the US. Thus, a franchise offering diabetic supplies is a growing market. As more people start their own businesses from home offices, the number of business services—such as bookkeeping, business coaching, and temporary help—are growing. Other growing areas are in fitness/wellness and in-home care/senior care. As schools close programs due to budget cuts, we realize there are now voids in such areas as children's fitness programs, tutoring, and after-school programs. Pet concepts remain strong because people will do anything for their pets, even in a weaker economy.

2. **Consumable products or ongoing services.** You want repeat customers. Commercial janitorial services, fitness centers, and hair salons, for example, all have repeat customers. On the other hand, a vacuum-cleaner franchise would have limited appeal since it could be years between purchases made by any one customer, and there's no assurance a customer would return to buy subsequent vacuum cleaners from you anyway. My mother bought a Kirby vacuum sweeper from a door-to-door salesman when I

was a teenager, and she used it for over ten years. The only repeat business they got from her came from an occasional repair or maintenance task.

3. **Perfect timing.** You want to be at the front of market trends so you're the first to take advantage of them. Pay attention to what trends are coming. One example is walk-in medical facilities—staffed by nurses as a way to replace the high cost of doctor visits—and that are located in stores such as Walmart. Drug testing, green technology and senior care are hot industries at the moment and will remain leaders for a while. The opposite is true for such franchises as Blockbuster. They are closing because movies on demand are now offered by Netflix and cable companies. The Borders bookstore chain closed because they did not adapt to the digital media that includes e-books.

4. **Strong compensation or attractive margins.** Pay attention to the money so you can recover your initial investment and make a big profit. There are profitable franchises and not-profitable ones. Conduct the same due diligence you learned about in chapter 8 on buying a business. Also, use an accountant and an attorney knowledgeable in franchises. Understand your specific franchise model; is it business-to-consumer (B2C) or business-to-business (B2B)? How is it performing? The fastest road to profitability is home-based B2B models, like direct mail and drug-testing services. You don't have the expensive overhead of a brick-and-mortar business, and you can ramp up quickly. Get this right and you are on solid ground; get it wrong and you are in quicksand.

5. **Powerful partnerships.** Evaluate the strength of the executive team running the franchise organization. When you buy a franchise, you're committing to the beginning of a long-term relationship,

which is very different from the relationship you have with a realtor when you buy a house. Once the house closes, the relationship stops. Once you buy a franchise, however, the relationship starts. So look at the executive team's business expertise and success, their ethics and values. You can discover a lot of information from the FDD and by calling current and former franchisees. Check for any complaints with the Better Business Bureau in the city and state of the franchisor's headquarters. Your state's Division of Securities or Office of Attorney General may also have more information. Dig as deep as you can.

6. **Unique products or exclusive technology.** How many competing companies or other franchisees sell similar products or services? For example, in New York City you will see a number of Starbucks stores that are so close to each other, they look as if they are next-door neighbors. That may be one of the reasons the company has closed more than two hundred units—because of the stores' market saturation. Quiznos lost its toasted-sandwich edge when such rivals as Subway began offering the same thing. If yours is a me-too product or service, how will you stand out? How many franchised and company-owned outlets are in your area? Does the franchise sell products or services that are easily available online or through a catalog?

The answers and ideas in each of the Six Key Ingredients (above) and the Real Deal Checklist (next) are to help you determine what data you want to find and what questions you need to ask. So keep researching and asking questions.

The Real Deal Checklist

We will continue to use the Real Deal Checklist introduced to you in chapter 7. Since green technology is a growing area in franchising, let's use it as an example in our checklist. Let's get more specific by looking at one segment of green technology: commercial janitorial services.

- **What:** The franchise is *practical* because of documented increases in pollution and respiratory illnesses from toxic cleaning products, which often make employees sick. The range of *applications* has already been determined by the franchisor cleaning commercial buildings. It is *immediately useable* because as soon as a customer has signed the contract, cleaning services can begin using current employees. The franchise name and brand will provide significant leverage for the franchisee to withstand the *competition* of the marketplace. This business opportunity is considered visual because people can *understand the benefits* of not getting sick from toxic cleaning products.
- **Who:** Customer profiles of who will buy from you include both individual businesses and building-complex landlords. The demographic is businesses that want to keep their employees and tenants healthy. The *location* of the customer is important because the franchise employees need to commute to the customers' building locations. *Repeat purchases* are aligned with *how long* the franchisee can keep its customers. The business can be boosted by word-of-mouth from one building owner to another. The *target market* is growing as people become more health and wellness conscience.

- *Why:* Business owners will buy the green services in order to meet the *need* to keep their employees and customers healthier by eliminating the *pain* of toxic cleaning products. Landlords can meet *unmet needs* by creating a unique market difference when they offer green cleaning services. *Trends* are growing for products that are not toxic to people, pets, or the environment.

- *How:* The franchisor will have already developed the *delivery process;* you will have to follow it. For example, you will likely hire *employees* rather than independent contractors. The franchise already has a predetermined *Internet* presence. Depending on your franchise, you may develop personal, in-depth *relationships* or have a revolving door of customers. Even if it is a high-traffic franchise, your prospective customers will recognize the customer service advantage they'll have with a clean, well-cared-for facility. (For example, when I use drive-through for fast food, there are certain stores of one chain I avoid because the service is slow and the employees look like zombies. Yet other units within that same chain consistently offer fast service, hot food, and attentive employees.) Delivery is also important. For example, you may also have to acquire *warehouse* space for your product inventory or you may be able to get just-in-time delivery.

- *More:* The franchisor has already determined exactly what you can provide. You do not have the option to expand offerings or change technology, although the franchisor's business model might very well include *low- and moderate-priced services* to get customers in the door, with the opportunity to *sell* them on *higher-priced services* after they have sampled your product or service.

- **You:** You have already identified your *areas of expertise and strengths,* and you know what you are *missing.* The franchisor has determined the work that needs to be done; all you have to do is *insert yourself and others* into the plan.

As you can see, buying a franchise is more straightforward than starting a company. And it has more resources available to you because the franchisor has already developed all of the processes necessary for a successful business. Thus, it's not surprising that the franchisor has very specific rules on what you can and cannot do to change anything.

Trust your own common sense about those franchises that are economically sensitive; the ones that, when the economy goes down, so do sales. High-end examples include retail stores, clothing lines, and expensive food and restaurants. You are a consumer, so what would you immediately stop buying if you had to reduce your spending? Look five years out—not five months—as you evaluate your options.

Shopping for a Franchise

Once you decide a franchise may be a good Plan B option for you, it's time to go shopping. There are several ways to do this, including Internet research, attending a franchise event, and working with a business or franchise broker. You will also want to include a visit to the franchise headquarters as part of your due diligence. Remember, you are turning over thousands—maybe millions—of dollars, and you need to meet and know the people behind the brand.

Internet ad portals provide a directory of some of the franchise opportunities organized by industry, location, and investment. The most popular include:

FranchiseGator.com

FranchiseSolutions.com

FranchiseDirect.com

Franchising.com

BizBuySell.com

Entrepreneur.com

—Peter Carlson, entrepreneur, franchise broker[17]

Internet Search

The Internet is filled with ad portal websites that let you find, sort, and filter franchise options. No one website will represent all possible franchises, so you will need to visit several of them. You can sort by investment amount, industry, and location (typically by state).

Start by getting a list of the franchises that meet your requirements. When you're at one of these ad portal websites, you will typically fill out an online form, and the information you requested will be forwarded to the franchisor you are interested in. Each company has its own process for contacting you; some will e-mail, others will call you, many will do both. You can also look up a franchisor's contact information and call the company directly. The franchisor will provide not only ownership information but also the type of support and training, financing options, and locations that are available to help you as you begin looking at a specific franchise.

Shopping at a Franchise Exposition

Events such as trade shows, expos, forums, and conferences are all designed to help you see and compare various franchise businesses and to meet face to face with the people associated with franchises you might be interested in. Through seminars and franchisor discussions, the events offer a productive way to learn a lot in a short period of time.

Franchise events are similar to trade shows with vendors, displays, tables, and marketing material. These events are scheduled throughout the year and in a variety of locations, so consider attending one or two. There is typically a small fee to attend.

Get a list in advance of the franchisors that will be at the event. Determine which ones are of interest to you and then start your research by going online, talking to franchisees in your area, and getting the FDDs. You can expect the event's seminars will provide more information on such topics as financing, the pros and cons of buying a franchise, franchise laws, social media, marketing, and growth.

Exhibitors attend so they can find and sign up new franchisees. They may offer you incentives to attend a promotional meeting to discuss the franchise in greater detail. These meetings can be another source of information and another opportunity to raise questions. Some of the exhibitors will be from the franchise headquarters; others may be recruiting for their area development or master/regional franchises. You will want to find out if they are recruiting for the franchisor, for their own territory, or for their own brokerage business so you will understand their agenda. As long as you know what each person stands to gain from talking to you, you can take that into consideration as you interact with exhibitors.

Using a Franchise Broker

We spent time in chapter 8 discussing business brokers and how they can help you to buy a business. In this chapter, we will first evaluate working with a franchise broker and then with a franchise advisor. In the "Finding a Franchise Broker" section later in this chapter, you'll see a list of questions to ask when you contact either or both of these professionals. There is also a section on franchise advisors and how to find them.

Unfortunately, there is no certification required to become a franchise broker. Some of them work for themselves and others work for the franchisor. The brokers in business for themselves can represent up to two hundred different franchisors, which is only 5%-10% of the market. Since brokers will only steer you to what they have to offer, the number and variety of franchises you'll discuss are limited. On that same note, it is estimated less than 50% of franchisors use brokers to represent them. Strong franchisors, such as Subway and McDonald's, don't use brokers; you will need to contact them directly. Small, start-up franchises will sign up buyers themselves, in part to ensure the buyers are a good fit for their business.[18]

With all of that said, working with a respected, knowledgeable franchise broker is still a good idea. For starters, the broker can help you sort through some of the types of franchises available (although try to have a feel for what type you're interested in before you contact a broker). Since one firm cannot possibly offer all of the franchises available, it's best to contact multiple brokers representing the various brands you're interested in. You may be dealing with two or three brokers, each representing different franchisors, so make it clear that you will conduct your own due diligence on the franchise broker and on the franchisor. If the broker pressures you to work with him or her exclusively, end the relationship.

Below are several advantages and disadvantages for using a franchise broker. In addition, you'll see a section on how to choose a franchise broker, what questions to ask, and what can tip you off if this person is a bad choice. As with all of your business choices, you will also want the help of an accountant and attorney with franchise expertise before you finalize a purchase.

Advantages of Using a Franchise Broker

Below is a list of specific benefits of working with a broker. Even though the broker will offer you only the franchises he or she represents, feel free to use the broker's services to gather information and answer questions.

- **Help narrow choices.** Brokers can help identify the types of franchises that match your interests and skills. Because brokers typically work with specific franchisors, they should have an in-depth understanding of each of them.
- **Evaluate options.** Once you have narrowed your list to certain types of franchises, brokers can help you evaluate specific franchise options.
- **Prepare paperwork.** Brokers often help you complete the franchisor's applications and paperwork, as well as gather and prepare the details required for any financing you may need.
- **No cost to you.** The broker's fee(s) are paid by the franchisor (if it's a new unit) or by the seller of an existing franchise that is already for sale. There is no cost to you, and the purchase price won't be any more expensive if you use a broker.
- **Increased objectivity.** Brokers are less emotionally involved in the outcome, so they can think more clearly and objectively as you become more committed to a purchase. But, of course, you have to be willing to listen.

Questions to ask other franchisees about a specific broker:

- Would you work with this person again?
- Did the broker help you find a franchise that was a good match?
- Did they correctly represent everything?
- What do you wish the broker would have told you but didn't?
- Did the broker recommend the types of franchises that would be both the best and worse matches for you?

—JOEL LIBAVA, FRANCHISE ADVISOR, FRANCHISE SELECTION SPECIALISTS, INC.[19]

Disadvantages of Using a Franchise Broker

Since brokers will only recommend what they sell, here are a few cautions you need to know.

- **Commission driven.** Brokers don't get paid until the sale is closed. This is the same as a car dealership; no sale, no commission. Not surprisingly, they are motivated to close your deal.
- **Questionable recommendations.** Some brokers represent any franchisor willing to pay them a commission for a sale, so it's possible the broker may recommend a failing operation. This is where it's vital you conduct your own due diligence. Chapter 8 guided you through looking at the finances of a business you're considering purchasing, and there is specific information on due diligence for franchise purchases later in this chapter.
- **Commission incentives.** Some brokers are paid a percentage of the selling price and will automatically lean toward concepts with the highest commission. Be sure to find out what the broker's commission is for each franchise they recommend. It could be the one with the highest broker commission is your best choice, but you will still want to know.
- **Some lie.** Unfortunately, some brokers lie about income, earnings, sales, expenses, and profits. This is another reason why you must complete your own due diligence with your accountant and attorney.

The advantages and disadvantages of using a franchise broker are similar to those for working with a business broker to buy a business, as we discussed in chapter 8.

Brokers can be a great asset, but you'll still need to conduct your own research and due diligence.

Let's look at how to evaluate brokers to ensure they are reputable.

Finding a Franchise Broker

Now that you know the good and the bad about using a broker, here is more information on how to find a reputable one.

It is easy to conduct an Internet search using the term *franchise broker*. The problem is that anyone can call themselves one, yet have no experience or successful processes in place for working with buyers.

Interview the broker before you begin the actual franchise-purchasing consultation process. See if you can make a connection with the broker. Look for someone who will take all the time you need to answer your questions. Is there a chemistry match? You will be spending hours, weeks, and even months working with this person to find and buy a franchise.

> "It is not uncommon for a franchise broker to work with 50–200 franchisors.
>
> Some are very selective about who they represent; others are not."
>
> —ED TEIXEIRA, FRANCHISE KNOW HOW, LLC; AUTHOR, *HOW TO BUY A FRANCHISE*[20]

Interview Questions for Evaluating Brokers

These are some of the core questions you should ask during your first conversation. Listen for the broker's depth of knowledge and understanding of the ins and outs of franchising. Remember, it's important to find someone you would enjoy working with, since the franchise-purchasing process will take months. It's exciting and fun, but it's a lot of work too. Find someone who will help you work through the tough spots and who is knowledgeable and trustworthy.

> "Most brokers work as franchisees or independent contractors with franchise broker groups. Some of the more prominent are:
>
> FranChoice
>
> The Franchise Alliance
>
> Frannet
>
> The Business Alliance
>
> The Entrepreneur Source
>
> Request performance results for your business segment and investment level. For example, home-based senior care at a $75,000 investment level."
>
> —ED TEIXEIRA, FRANCHISE KNOW HOW, LLC; AUTHOR, HOW TO BUY A FRANCHISE [20]

1. **What is your background in franchising?** You want someone who has successfully run a franchise(s) and/or has been on the corporate staff of one. The more business experience the broker has, the better, because he or she will know what to look for. You also want to know who are some of the broker's clients, so you know who they typically represent. Look for highly visible franchise concepts. Remember, you can work with multiple brokers at the same time.

2. **How many years have you been a full-time broker?** Since franchise contracts are typically for ten years, you want someone who has been in the business for at least three to five years. You also want someone who has made this a profession instead of someone who dabbles in it.

3. **Have you written articles or books, or been quoted in the media as an expert on franchising?** You are checking out this person's depth of knowledge and amount of initiative.

4. **Are you working in any other businesses?** Find out if the broker is dealing exclusively with the franchise industry. If not, this may create a problem if the broker wants to present other business opportunities to you instead of a good franchise. For example, the broker may try to convince you to become a franchise broker or offer you a non-franchise business they represent or are involved in.

5. **How many franchises have you sold?** You want someone who has processed at least fifty franchise purchases. That number ensures they have enough experience to know which things can go wrong and

to have learned from their mistakes. You also want a list of at least fifteen franchisees who have bought from this person within the last three years so you can get references from those franchisees. Ask them what it was like to work with this person, how he or she was of help, if the broker misrepresented anything about the franchisor, and if the franchisee would work with this person again.

6. **How many franchisors do you represent?** Who are they? How do you decide which franchisors to represent? Some brokers are very selective and represent only strong franchisors. Others will gladly add any franchisor who will pay a commission. It is not uncommon for brokers to work with 50–200 franchisors at one time.

7. **How will you select which franchisors to present to me?** What are your selection criteria? The broker should talk about taking time to learn about you, your business background, strengths and weaknesses, interests, and the investment you can make. Some brokers may have assessments for you to take to help identify the best type of franchise for you. The broker should also spend time learning why you are interested in a franchise and what your exit strategy might be. If the broker starts making franchise recommendations before learning all of this, you don't want to work with that person.

8. **How long does buying a franchise take?** Since it can easily take months to find the franchisors you like and to conduct your due diligence, you want someone who is going to take time to help you make a good choice. If the consultant gets miffed when you don't jump on the first three or four offered to you, you may not want to continue working with this person. If he or she offers you franchises you are not interested in or that are out

of your price range, they haven't been listening to you. Find another broker.

9. **How do you conduct your due diligence?** If the broker does not understand the process or gives you questionable answers to your financial questions, then drop them. Keep in mind you have learned a lot about business and due diligence by reading this book. Although a broker can't know everything, you can expect him or her to have solid business knowledge and understanding that will truly help you.

10. **Have you ever been sued by a franchisor or franchisee?** The United States is a litigious culture, so this person may have been sued and yet still be good at what he or she does. But if there has been more than one lawsuit, find out about the specific reasons for each one. Then you can decide if they have just too many problems and you don't want to work with them.

11. **Have you ever told anyone that he or she is not a good match for franchising?** Would you have the courage to tell me if that was the case? You want to know if this person is only in it for the money or if he has the integrity to say something to you if you're clearly not suited to be a franchise owner.

Franchise Advisors Work for You

Franchise advisors are similar to franchise brokers in that an advisor acts as a mentor and coach, and there is no certification required to call yourself one. Some advisors are inexpensive but don't offer much value. Others are expensive and guide you through each step of the selection, buying, and negotiation process. They will also typically have experts they work with such as bankers, attorneys, and accountants that can be a resource to you too.

> "Franchise advisors work for you for a fee. They are not paid on commission like brokers are.
>
> An advisor is an advocate to make sure franchise ownership is right for you, and to help you with the research and finding funding and an attorney before buying a franchise."
>
> —JOEL LIBAVA, FRANCHISE ADVISOR, FRANCHISE SELECTION SPECIALISTS, INC.[22]

But there are a few important differences between these franchise advisors and the franchise brokers we discussed in the previous section.

Advisors work for you for a fee that you pay them, so they will unquestionably represent your best interests. This is the same idea as the for-fee financial planner you pay to give you the best financial-planning recommendations, instead of steering you only to their company's financial products.

Franchise advisors' focus is to make sure franchise buyers know that there is inherent risk to buying a franchise business; success is not guaranteed. Because you pay them a fee, they will not steer you toward failing franchises with higher commission rates for them—they're not taking a commission. Nor are they incented to close a deal, but rather to ensure you are a good match for franchise ownership and conduct your due diligence. Advisors can also help determine if a broker you may already be working with has your best interest in mind.

Franchise advisors don't have any of the disadvantages brokers do, and yet they have most of the same advantages: they help narrow your choices and evaluate options, and they are more objective. Because their success is based on you making the right decisions, you should expect them to be candid about whether you are a good match...or not well suited to owning a franchise.

Interview potential advisors and ask them the same questions listed earlier in this chapter for brokers. Look for advisors who have been in the franchise business for over fifteen years, although twenty is better.

Finding a Franchise Advisor

There are a variety of sources to help you find expert franchise advisors. Certainly the experts I sought help from for this chapter can be of assistance to you, and their contact information is in the notes at the end of this chapter.

Other helpful sources include:

- Small Business Development Centers (SBDCs) associated with the SBA. SBDCs provide advice to business owners and may have experts about franchising too. Find your nearest SBDC at www.SBA.gov.

- SCORE offers advice for low cost or no fee. The advisors are typically retired business executives, some of who come from the franchise industry. You can find them online at their website, www.SCORE.org. Many SCOREs are associated with local chambers of commerce.

- American Association of Franchises and Dealers (AAFD). This organization represents franchisees and provides useful advice and resources. Visit them at www.AAFD.org.

Conduct Your Due Diligence

It is your job to conduct your own due diligence on the franchises you are interested in, although your accountant and attorney will be of help to you.

Early in the process, the franchisor will provide the government-mandated Franchise Disclosure Document

(FDD) to you and will probably send some brochures or videos as well. You will likely have one or more conversations with someone from the franchisor's development team and, if you are both still interested, you will be invited to a meeting with the franchisor (sometimes called a Discovery Day) to learn more about the business concept.

Just as you learned in chapter 8, analyzing the financial performance will occupy 80%-90% of your due-diligence time. The FDD, for example, provides twenty-three categories of information. Technically, the franchisor needs to provide it only ten days before you sign a contract, but you'll certainly want to begin your due diligence a lot sooner than that.

The FDD includes the information you need to get started, but it won't contain all of what you need. You can find a sample FDD on the Federal Trade Commission's website at www.FTC.gov.[23]

One area in which you'll need to spend more time is finding out the earnings of individual franchises. Franchisors are not required to make earnings claims, but if they do, there has to be a reasonable basis for these claims and they have to provide you with a document that substantiates them. This substantiation includes the bases and assumptions upon which these claims are made. Make sure you get and review the earnings claims document. This is where your accountant will be of great help to you.

But back to the FDD. Here are a few of its twenty-three sections:

- **Business experience and background of company officers.** You are looking for backgrounds that include running successful businesses and franchises. The FDD will show each person's most recent five years, and more if the background includes franchise experience. You want officers with experience operating a franchise(s), so they understand what it is like to be a franchisee. If they have no experience as a franchisee, they may or may not be able to make the decisions that will best serve you.

- **Any current or pending litigation.** You want to determine if there is a pattern of the franchisor suing the franchisees, which could be a sign of a badly behaving franchisor. Or if you notice a lot of lawsuits by franchisees, you will want to be careful here too. A quick Internet search can provide enough information to get you started.

- **Initial investment.** This will show you the initial cost of buying the franchise, which is technically the trade name and systems. In addition, there will be other fees such as royalty payments, and training and advertising fees. There will be other costs too, such as real estate, equipment, signs, and inventory. The FDD will provide an estimate of the total cost for buying and opening a franchise.

- **List of all franchise owners currently in the system.** This is critical to analyzing the profitability of franchises. The FDD does not provide a breakdown on the earnings or profitably of individual franchisees; instead, the FDD typically provides averages, which can be misleading. Using averages can make the franchisor look more successful than it is. Talk with each franchisee to find out individual earnings. Their earnings aren't a guarantee that yours will be the same, but at least you'll have a realistic

> "Franchisees of the chain are free to provide sales and profitability figures, but franchisors and their sales agents are not."
>
> — SEAN KELLY, PRESIDENT, IDEAFARM; PUBLISHER OF FRANCHISEMARKETING.COM[24]

idea of what is possible. Talk with as many franchisees as you can. This is where your investment of time will give you a big payoff because you will learn a lot more about the profitability ranges of various franchises.

- **List of all franchise owners that have left the system in the past twelve months.** Contact as many of these people as you can and find out why they left. If you discover most of them lost money or did not feel supported, you will certainly want to think carefully before proceeding with this franchisor.
- **Obligations of the franchisor and of the franchisee.** This spells out what you can expect from the franchisor. It also spells out the obligations and conditions you must meet to keep the franchise.

Your homework during this process is to talk with as many existing franchisees as you can to learn as much as possible about being a franchisee of this system. Most of those people you contact will talk freely with you. You may be asked to sign a non-disclosure agreement before they will answer any questions so they can ensure their personal information is not shared—this is fine and par for the course.

If the franchisees feel poorly supported, they will tell you. If the majority are happy, that's a sign that you may be too. Take the time you need to call as many current and former franchisees as you can so that you will have a number of opinions to use in your analysis.

Ask the franchisees these questions and any others that are suitable to your situation and the franchise:

- Are you happy with your choice of franchisors?
- Would you buy the same franchise again?

- Did the franchisor's training adequately prepare you to run your franchise unit?
- Were the start-up costs quoted accurately?
- Do you feel you've received ongoing support from the franchisor?
- What problems have they not fixed yet?
- Is your franchise unit profitable or on track to make a profit?
- What were your revenues the last two years?

Now let's learn more about buying an existing franchise rather than a new one.

Should You Buy a New or an Existing Franchise?

Just like buying an existing business is less risky than starting one, you may be better off buying an operating franchise rather than starting from scratch. A new storefront franchise can cost $200,000–$300,000 to open. An existing unit with good cash flow can be acquired for about the same cost as opening a new one, and sometimes less. You also don't have the headaches of site selection, construction, staffing, or getting those first customers through the door.

If you are considering buying an existing franchise, which is called a *franchise resell,* be sure you're thorough in your due diligence. Like the recommendations in chapter 8 on buying a business, you need to understand why the owners are selling the business. It could be because it is not profitable, or maybe the owners are burned out, or they want to retire. Find out if there are some good, logical reasons they are selling it.

However, most franchises today are sold because of poor profitability, or because the franchisee has gotten himself in trouble with the franchisor. Running into trouble with a food franchisor, for example, could mean the franchisee has not met sanitation standards and now has to renovate the kitchen. If the franchisee doesn't want to spend the $75,000–$100,000 to buy new ovens or equipment, he or she might decide to sell it instead. Or perhaps it's in a bad location, or it is simply a bad franchisor with poor support and systems. Find out all the dirty little secrets during your due diligence, so you can make the right decision later.

Franchise brokers are paid to sign up new franchisees, so they are not usually going to present you with an existing one. However, franchise advisors will. If you want to buy an existing franchise, your process will be very similar to that of buying a business in chapter 8. You also need to ensure that there are no obligations after you buy the existing franchise, such as a requirement to renovate if the business is a storefront. For example, if a new franchise is $200,000, and you can buy a good existing one for $170,000, then you have a great price and a great deal as long as there are no existing obligations.

Wrap Up

You now have the good and bad news about buying a franchise, as well as the advantages and disadvantages. We applied the Six Key Ingredients and the Real Deal Checklist to a variety of franchises. We covered the four types of franchise models, as well as the restrictions and controls the franchisors typically impose on its franchisees.

You learned how to find franchisors and what to look for in one that's a good fit for you. You also learned how to find, evaluate, and use franchise brokers and advisors. You were introduced to the government-mandated Franchise Disclosure Document (FDD), and you know that just like when you're buying a business, most of your due diligence will be to analyze the financial information.

You now know more about franchises than at least 75% of the people who have actually bought one. Your chances of success will be greatly improved if you use the specific recommendations in this chapter should you choose the franchise path for your Plan B.

Network marketing is the fourth of the four Plan B options, and we will explore it in the next chapter. As with each of the first three options, you will get the good and bad news as well as the advantages and disadvantages of this particular path. We will clear up many of the myths and misconceptions that are rampant in the network marketing industry. You will also learn the most common types of products and services sold and how to select a network marketing company. We will, of course, apply the Six Key Ingredients as well as the Real Deal Checklist to various offerings. You will learn two different ways to approach your business, what two of the typical compensation plans look like, how to conduct your own due diligence, and how to select the up-line organization that best meets your needs.

Notes

1   Ed Teixeira
    president, Franchise Know How, LLC
    author, *How to Buy a Franchise
    and The Franchise Buyer's Manual*
    www.franchiseknowhow.com

2   Peter Carlson
    entrepreneur, franchise broker, Sunbelt
    pcarlson@sunbeltnetwork.com

3   Sean Kelly
    "Lies, Damn Lies, and Franchise Statistics," ac-
    cessed September 2011
    www.FranchiseMarketing.com
    Sean Kelly is president of IdeaFarm, a franchise
    consulting firm, and the publisher of
    FranchiseMarketing.com

4   John Lucht
    "A $500,000 Thank You," Memos from John news-
    letter for members of www.RiteSite.com, June 22,
    2010
    John Lucht is the founder and owner of RiteSite.
    com,a career transition company for corporate
    executives. He is also the author of *Rites of Passage
    at $100,000 to $1 Million+: Your Insider's Lifetime
    Guide to Executive Job-Changing and Faster Career
    Progress in the 21st Century.*

5   Ed Teixeira
    The Franchise Buyer's Manual
    See also the 2007 Economic Census Franchise
    Report, which was produced in cooperation with the
    International Franchise Association (IFA).

6   "CURVES Franchise Lawsuit Settlements"
    Unhappy Franchisee.com, September 30, 2010
    www.unhappyfranchisee.com/curves-franchise-
    lawsuit-settlements/

7   "Franchise Brokers: Why Invest in a Franchise?"
    ProfitStreet, accessed 2012
    www.profitstreet.com

8   "What is a Franchiser?"
    wiseGeek, accessed 2012
    www.wisegeek.com/what-is-a-franchiser.htm

9   "FAQs of Franchising, Answers to the 19 Most Com-
    monly Asked Questions about Franchising; Question
    19: Are There Any Current Trends in Franchising?"
    International Franchise Association
    www.franchise.org/franchiseesecondary.
    aspx?id=10008

10 "Census Bureau's First Release of Comprehensive Franchise Data Shows Franchises Make Up More Than 10 Percent of Employer Businesses" September 14, 2010 www.census.gov/newsroom/releases/archives/economic_census/cb10-141.html

11 Joel Libava
franchise advisor
Franchise Selection Specialists, Inc.
and The Franchise King®
www.thefranchiseking.com

12 Ed Teixeira
in discussion with the author, September 2011

13 Libava

14 Ed Teixeira
How to Buy a Franchise and The Franchise Buyer's Guide

15 Peter Carlson
see also "4 Business Models of Franchising"
Franchises Made Simple
www.franchisesmadesimple.com/4-business-models-of-franchising

16 Ed Teixeira
How to Buy a Franchise and The Franchise Buyer's Guide

17 Carlson

18 Ibid.

19 Libava

20 Ed Teixeira
How to Buy a Franchise and The Franchise Buyer's Guide

21 Ibid

22 Libava

23 "Buying a Franchise: A Consumer Guide"
Bureau of Consumer Protection Business Center
Federal Trade Commission
http://business.ftc.gov/documents/inv05-buying-franchise-consumer-guide
February 2008

24 Kelly, "Lies"

CHAPTER 10

The Real Deal about Network Marketing

NETWORK MARKETING is a simple, straightforward form of distributing (i.e., selling) the products or services of a company to an end user. Instead of using a traditional retail system, the company has determined that their offerings are best sold through individuals who can personalize the sales process and create repeat customers. Because a large part of the retail distribution chain is eliminated, the cost of distribution is lower. Thus, the public theoretically receives higher quality offerings at the same or better prices.

It has been estimated there are almost eighty-eight million network marketing salespeople worldwide and fifteen million of those are located in the United States. The total global sales are estimated at $141 billion, with 24% (or more than $28 billion) made in the United States.[1] The industry has been around for a very long time. One of the oldest US network marketing companies, Avon Products, was founded in 1886.[2]

Network marketing is also referred to as *multi-level marketing (MLM)*, *referral marketing*, or *direct sales*. However, direct sales is not an accurate description, as you will see later in this chapter.

This is the fourth of the four ways to create a Plan B. Here again, you will use all that you learned about yourself in chapters 2 and 5 to determine if this option is a good match for you. We will also apply the Six Key Ingredients from chapter 6 and the Real Deal Checklist from chapter 7. And, of course, you will learn the good and bad news about network marketing, as well as its advantages and disadvantages.

I have also included specific questions to ask yourself to determine your interest level. This chapter includes a section on how to conduct your due diligence on network marketing companies, and how doing so is different than what you would do if you were buying a company or a franchise. This chapter also contains a profile of the type of people you will want to work with in your network marketing team because their skills and abilities will be important to you. Lastly, this chapter clarifies the confusion some people have if they believe network marketing is the same as a pyramid or Ponzi scheme; legitimate network marketing companies are *not*.

Briefly, the premise of network marketing is the development of a network of people, called *distributors,* who are paid on a commission-only basis. The larger the network, the more products and services are sold. Think about a food manufacturer who has distributors that sell its products directly to end users, such as restaurants and grocery stores. Network marketing works the same way. The company develops and delivers the offerings; your job is to sell them.

US network marketing industry statistics:

- $28+ billion in sales
- 16 million sellers
- 80%+ are female
- 90%+ are part-time

—2010 Fact Sheet, Direct Selling Association[3]

The attraction of network marketing is the low cost of entry and the promise of eventually building the business to the point your commissions are bigger than your Plan A paycheck. In theory, if you build a big enough group and have enough repeat customers, you can quit your Plan A job, and, through this business, have lifetime income much like you would a pension. It is called *residual,* or *passive income* and is further defined below.

Let's define the terms we will use in this chapter.

- A *distributor* or *independent distributor* is typically what you are called when you sign up with a network marketing company. You work on commission-only but are eligible for bonuses. You earn perks—such as the use of leased cars and trips paid for by the company—based on sales volume and recruiting new distributors.

- You are a *down-line* to the distributor who signed you up as part of his or her team.

- Your *up-line* is the distributor who signed you up and whose team you are on. This person is not your boss—he or she does not hold you accountable for your activities. This person didn't hire you and is not paying you a wage or salary. Instead, the up-line's job is to mentor, coach, and train you. A good up-line will match your energy; they will work as hard as you do. Their attention will be on you as well as on recruiting other distributors and making sales to customers. You may also have relationships with their up-lines, sometimes three or more levels up. Because the up-lines get paid in part based on your sales volume, they have a vested interest in your success. To picture this structure, think about a division or department within a traditional company: there are layers of management above your boss. They all

"If you are thinking about starting a business or buying one and haven't run one before, network marketing is the perfect place to start. You will build your skills and find out if you have what it takes to run your own business."

—JEFF PIERSALL, PRESIDENT AND COFOUNDER, SCB MEDIA; FORMER NETWORK MARKETING TOP-SELLING DISTRIBUTOR want you to perform well because that is how everyone succeeds and makes money.

- *Cross-lines* are those distributors who are peers to you, much as coworkers in different departments in a Plan A-type company each have their own responsibilities. Sometimes cross-lines work together on projects, but mainly they stay focused on their own jobs.

- *Residual* or *passive income* is the income that continues after your initial effort. It does not require your continuing, direct involvement. Examples of residual income include the cash provided by real estate rentals, the interest or dividends paid on investments, the royalties from a book or from licensing a patent, and income from pensions. In the case of network marketing, it is the commissions paid on services that are renewed or products that are repurchased on a regular basis.

- The terms *end users* and *customers* are used interchangeably to refer to the people buying the products or services.

- *Recruit* means you will find other people you want to work with you as your down-line. It is the same thing as recruiting employees for a business, except your recruits' compensation is commission-only.

- *Sponsor* is what you become after a prospective down-line signs up with you. As the sponsor, you will mentor them through the sign-up process, get their websites set up, and show them how to conduct business.

- *Direct sales* pays commission on the sale of products and/or services. There is no compensation for recruiting new distributors, which is a common component of compensation in network marketing.

Giving You the Real Deal Guide on Network Marketing

The *good news* about network marketing is that it is a simple business concept. By choosing a company that matches you and your interests, you'll have a natural group of potential customers who will be interested in buying what you recommend. For example, if you are a personal trainer or a health and wellness coach, signing up with a network marketing company that has high-quality vitamins and supplements is a natural match. If you are a hair stylist, then signing up with a company with anti-aging skin care or cosmetic products is a match.

The initial investment in network marketing is small compared to the other three Plan B options, but it will require the same hard work to make it a success. Also, based on the design of the compensation plan, you can develop a large number of repeat customers that, over time, will bring you residual (i.e., passive) income.

The *bad news* is network marketing is about selling to end users and recruiting others to sell and recruit too. Some people feel they have no idea how to sell or are reluctant to try to approach others. To find one successful down-line, for example, you will likely have to recruit at least ten people, because nine may quit. So this is about your ability to handle rejection and keeping your *why* in mind.

Also, because you are your own boss and don't have the imposed structure of running a store, you will need to develop the discipline to manage your time, make sales calls or hold events, and follow through with those interested in buying your product and/or service or in joining your team. For new distributors, it may seem like everyone is potentially your customer, so you may feel you are always under pressure to be prospecting.

Additionally, the person recruiting you to be part of his or her team may not have the skills and/or knowledge to help you become successful. This up-line person may be new themselves and quit after six months or a year, leaving you to work with their up-line and deal with any fallout.

Let's explore how John Whitaker, who had moved successfully through several careers, found network marketing was a good match for him. No matter how successful you have been, this Plan B option may still of interest and help to you at different times in your life.

> "I grew up watching my dad work in the coal mines of West Virginia. That made me realize I needed to be doing something different. I decided that education was my way out. I earned the money to go to college by working part-time in the mines and the lumber mill, which just strengthened my resolve not to be trapped there. After graduation, I joined the military. They paid for my master's degrees, so I had some options when I got out. After twenty-three years, I retired as a lieutenant colonel and decided to reinvent myself by running international businesses in Europe. As a CEO, I had to increase

sales and improve operations in each one of the businesses and quickly learned how to do it.

"After a while, I got tired of dealing with overbearing management boards and making other people rich. I had been paid very well but knew I would have to reinvent myself again. I resigned and moved to Florida. After looking around, I invested a half-million dollars in a nutrition store and started a diabetic-supply company on the side. If that wasn't enough to keep me busy, I created a health-talk radio show which promoted healthy choices and my other two businesses at the same time. I was busy and life was pretty good until the hurricanes. They severely damaged my store and then the economy crashed. I needed cash flow—a Plan B."

John had done all the right things: gotten a great education, worked hard and diligently, and made career decisions that were a great match with his personal interests. But then he was hit with a double whammy—hurricanes and the recession. Fortunately, his journey continued...

"I had already joined a network marketing company because its high-quality supplements worked well in my store, and the lucrative commission plan was very attractive. I had only four hours on Wednesday mornings to work on building this business. It turned out that finding this company was good thing, too. When I had to eventually close my store, it was losing over $7,500 a month because my sales no longer covered the cost of running the business. If it wasn't for the network marketing income I was getting from product new sales, new distributors, and customers reordering, I would have found myself in a very difficult situation right now."

Network marketing was not a career John had had in mind, yet he has now worked for more than seven years to build his network marketing business and has over two thousand distributors across the United States and in twenty-eight countries. He doesn't have employees or overhead to worry about. By his fourth year he had earned over a million dollars in commission. By the sixth year, he crossed the two-million-dollar-earner mark. He loves the freedom and the relationships with his peers and some of the down-lines that network marketing have given him. As a leader in the company, he enjoys many perks—such as luxurious cruises and trips to Paris—awarded as incentives to top performers.

As with each of the Plan B options, there are advantages and disadvantages. Of course, since this is the *real deal guide*, I will give you both.

Network Marketing Advantages

- **World-class branding.** Name recognition can go a long way to introducing end users to what you offer. It's just easier when prospects have heard of your company or even used its products or services in the past. Avon, Amway, and Mary Kay have been in business for decades and are well-known brand names.
- **Proven systems.** The product or service has been researched and developed; the accounting and commission systems are in place; shipping and tracking, customer service, and product reordering and returns are processed by the company. Like a franchise in chapter 9, a network marketing company is a

> "Mary Kay and her company became well known for recognizing and rewarding her top-selling distributors with a leased pink Cadillac."
>
> —KATHLEEN RICH-NEW, BUSINESS CONSULTANT, SPEAKER, EXECUTIVE COACH, CLARITY WORKS CONSULTING; AUTHOR, *PLAN B*

turnkey operation, and it has been repeatedly tested and refined.

- **Training.** There is a lot to learn about how to develop relationships, how to recruit other distributors to join you, and how to sell and service your customers. You will need to know what training the company offers and what the distributor you are talking to and his or her up-line can do to support you. Take your time and don't be rushed to sign up after a dazzling presentation and a compelling sign-up pitch. If you sign up with an up-line and later discover you don't want to work with that person, you may have to become inactive for several months before you can switch to a new up-line. That means you lose your momentum and may lose your customers. If you have any down-lines, they will have to do the same thing or you will lose them too. So think through this decision carefully, and keep reading!

- **Customer and distributor support.** Customer service and distributor support play a critical role in answering questions and resolving problems for you, your down-lines, and your customers. There is usually a toll-free number and e-mail access for them to use, which means the companies' experts solve problems so you can focus on selling and recruiting.

- **Unlimited expansion capability.** You can work from any location at whatever time you choose, recruit from any country the company operates in, and grow as big and as fast as your abilities allow you—typically at low or no additional fees. This is different than a franchise, which usually requires buying a new unit or territory to expand.

- **Low barrier of entry and limited risk.** Because of the low investment—from a few hundred dollars to a few thousand—essentially anyone can join a

> In addition to Avon, two of the other top three top US network marketing companies have been around for a long time:
>
> - Mary Kay was founded in 1963
> - Amway was founded in 1959
>
> —"THE TOP 25 NETWORK MARKETING COMPANIES," NEXERA LLC[4]

team. High levels of business education or technical knowledge are rarely required. Because your investment level is low, if you decide to quit you will not be financially ruined, which could happen when buying a business or a franchise.

- **Out earn the people who came in prior to you.** In legitimate network marketing companies, it does not matter where you are in the organization or when you started. Your commission checks are related to your selling and distributor-recruiting abilities. So if you are hearing such high-pressure tactics as "Get in on the ground floor" or "This is the chance of a lifetime," walk away. (There is more later in this chapter on what to look for in a network marketing company.)

- **True equal opportunity.** Your success is all about you. No one is holding you back or making you feel inferior. You alone hold your success in your hands by your willingness to be coachable, and your ability to learn how to sell and sponsor others, and your commitment to the business. It will typically take at least three to five years of consistent and diligent work for you to build a solidly profitable team.

- **Success is labeled and recognized.** As you become more successful by having more sales from customers and/or your down-line distributors, you will earn *pin titles*, as they're often called. The titles are often such names as gold, ruby, diamond, and blue diamond, or they're business titles, such as executive or director, or they tie in with the company's products or services in a clever and memorable way. Each progressive level is recognized internally as representing a higher sales-volume level. Along with advanced titles comes a higher percentage of commission, which can start at a low rate of 5% and increase up to 35%

for the top pin titles. Other tangible rewards can include the use of a high-end, leased car for the year and lavish trips with other successful distributors who have worked hard to enjoy the same rewards.

You now know the advantages of network marketing, so let's explore the disadvantages.

Network Marketing Disadvantages

As with each Plan B option, you want to thoroughly understand its negatives—or potential negatives.

- **Easy entry means a high drop-out rate.** The majority of distributors quit before they have achieved a desirable income. One reason is because they did not put down tens of thousands of dollars, so they take a lax, unfocused, and undisciplined approach to building the business. Another theory is that they did not understand the work required to sell the products and services to end users; or that these distributors don't want to sell to the extent that's necessary. Commissions will depend on the number of other distributors they can recruit in their down-line and how well the down-line performs, so that varies widely too. It is hard to find accurate statistics on the drop-out rate of distributors but it's estimated to be about 95%, with some of the dropouts only working enough to get their products for free.
- **Most people have never been trained and/or have limited natural selling abilities.** Selling is a foreign concept to many people who have only worked for others in traditional, non-sales jobs. If you are not comfortable in sales, then it's critical to find out what training the company offers. Some companies make a profit from their training, so you can except

to add training costs to your investment. Others companies charge just enough to cover their costs.

> "Do you want to make money? Can you learn? Selling is a learned a skill."
>
> — JOE PICI. COFOUNDER AND COO, PICI AND PICI, AUTHOR, *SELL NAKED ON THE PHONE AND SALES TRAINING*[5]

Also, find out about the sales background and ability of the person who wants to sign you up. Most network marketing companies do a poor job of providing you sufficient sales training, so ask a lot of questions and attend one of their training sessions as part of your due diligence. Be prepared to invest in yourself with outside training; it is a lifelong skill everyone can use. The boot camp training requirements of the military, for example, can last two to three months. My nephew joined the military in a specialized area that required seventeen weeks of training. One cable company, Bright House, trains their non-technical employees for three weeks before these new employees ever talk to a customer. The company's technical employees, on the other hand, train full-time for five weeks and then work with an experienced employee before they are allowed to work on their own. Like everyone in these examples, you will learn new skills and it will take time for you to master them, so be patient and keep your *why* in mind.

- **High failure rate of start-up network marketing companies.** New network marketing companies fail at the same rate as other start-up companies. The biggest money usually comes in year six or seven, when the company has shown they can stay in business, deliver the products, support their distributors and customers, and grow ethically. So the myth of being in on the ground floor of a start-up does not hold up statistically.

- **Confusing compensation plans.** Some compensation plans are straightforward: you have a minimum yearly purchase, and you can buy at wholesale, sell at retail and keep the difference. Others are confusing and hard to understand. For example, you may earn a different commission percentage at different pin levels and on different products, plus you might need a minimum sales volume each month in order to receive a check. Unless you are just looking for something fun to do, slow down until you thoroughly understand the compensation plan structure. I advocate this same advice for all of the Plan B options.

- **Hard-to-verify earnings claims.** Network marketing companies can provide you with an example of the level of compensation you can earn, but like weight loss spokespersons, they have achieved unusual results. One high-quality company's compensation plan shows you can be earning more than $500,000 a year when you have 12-14 top-selling down-lines. In interviews with some of the top-selling distributors, some are at the top because they went into a partnership with another distributor that was doing well. The partners each had six or seven top-selling down-lines and created a legal partnership to combine them into one team. The end results are that the partners get bigger commissions, make more money, and spread the workload. No one is usually willing to tell you behind-the-scene details like this.

- **Limited product or service offerings.** Some companies are a one-trick pony and have only one offering. Others offer questionable "lotions and potions" or "snake oil" that are simply overpriced products with no unique benefit. If there isn't robust product development, company acquisitions, or a strong research and development staff, then you have a limited selection of average offerings. Or if the offerings are easy to duplicate, your customers may choose

> "Of a direct-sales company's distributors, 80% will join based on emotion, because they have a dream.
>
> But if they don't quickly convert emotion into commitment and action, they will not be successful.
>
> Long-term commitment is one of the most important decisions required to be successful in any business."
>
> — JOHN WHITAKER, RETIRED MILITARY OFFICER, CORPORATE EXECUTIVE, TOP-SELLING NETWORK MARKETING DISTRIBUTOR

to buy them at Walmart instead of from you. Also, without a steady flow of innovation to grow your business, you will need to constantly find new end users for your products or services.

- **Market saturation.** Because you have an unlimited expansion capability, it is possible that a large number of distributors will be trying to sell to or recruit the same people you are. Witness the number of exotic health juices in recent years. However, market saturation may actually give you an advantage if you can offer higher customer service; end users may want to switch to you.

- **Needs to be built slowly.** Network marketing is all about momentum. The faster you build it, the faster you can lose it. The slower you build it, the more stable it's going to be. Don't pay attention to the people trotted out on stage that signed up six months ago and have 127 distributors. You probably won't see them in two years because they can't maintain that pace, and they have not built a stable team.

- **Noise about how bad network marketing is.** Although each of the Plan B options has a less-than-perfect success rate, there is a lot more noise (e.g., content on websites, blogs, and in articles) about how bad network marketing is. Just Google the name of any network marketing company and the word *scam,* and you will typically see a list of upset people. Look carefully, because you'll see most of these negative sites want to sell you a book, training materials, or a list of potential distributors; these sites have their own agendas!

There are generally four reasons you may find a lot more negative information about network marketing failures than you will on the other three Plan B options.

1. Since the cost is low to get into network marketing and it is low risk (you won't lose much money if you quit), there are a lot more people involved in it who just want to try it out. When they find out it is hard work or they aren't good at selling, they get angry, quit, and tell everyone about what a rip-off it is. This is quite different from someone who invests $300,000 to start a business or buy a franchise, and who will do whatever it takes to make it successful.

2. There is little real sales training; most of what exists is on the technical aspects of the product and how to recruit others. The network marketing business, however, is all about selling, so if you don't learn how to sell, you won't succeed.

3. The person doing the recruiting often sells the sizzle and not the steak. This recruiter typically talks only about the upside of earnings and recognition and not the downside of the years of consistent work it will take to be successful.

4. Success is measured by the sales volume of the top performers, not what the expectations are for the individual distributor. For example, research has shown that an extra $500 to $750 a month is the difference between paying the mortgage and losing a home to foreclosure. Buying a new car may then become possible and so does saving for a college education. Lower and more realistic earnings expectations could help keep more people engaged in the network company they've recently committed to.

Network Marketing: Ponzi Scheme, Pyramid Scheme or Path to Profit?

Let's address the sometimes questionable reputation associated with the industry, now that you have just reviewed its disadvantages. Like any other industry, only a few of its businesses have succeeded in a big way. For example, in the United States, only five network marketing companies have sales of more than $1 billion; they have been able to create products and services that customers want and will repeatedly buy. Already successful business executives are analyzing network marketing and see it as a growing and profitable industry. For example, Warren Buffett, a self-made billionaire, now owns six network marketing companies because of their growth and profitability. Real estate mogul Donald Trump has seen the same industry trends and has started one of his own. Both men, already highly successful, have analyzed the industry and seen its huge, potential growth and success.

Some people automatically reject the network marketing business model because they mistakenly think it is an illegal Ponzi or pyramid scheme. It is not. Let's pull back the curtain to understand the real deal about each of these areas.[7]

Ponzi schemes

Charles Ponzi duped thousands of New England residents into investing in a postage-stamp speculation scheme back in the 1920s. At a time when the annual interest rate for bank accounts was 5%, Ponzi promised investors that he could provide a 50% return in just ninety days. Ponzi initially bought a small number of international mail coupons to support his scheme, but quickly switched to using incoming investor funds to pay off earlier investors.

Bernard L. Madoff is serving a 150-year sentence in federal prison for orchestrating a multi-billion-dollar Ponzi scheme that swindled money from thousands of investors.

The term now refers to any investment design in which the early investors are paid off with money coming in from later ones. No products or services are sold. The only focus is to get as many investors as possible.

Pyramid schemes

The Federal Trade Commission (FTC) has defined pyramid schemes as plans that concentrate on the commissions earned for recruiting new distributors and that generally ignore the marketing and selling of products and services. For example, FUND AMERICA's founder was arrested because 90% of revenues came from selling distributorships and not from selling their products. This made it a pyramid scheme, and not a legitimate network marketing company.

Some indicators of a pyramid scheme include:

- *A large and required up-front investment.* Legitimate network marketing companies require only a low investment to become a distributor. Technically, you should be able to join for a few dollars. However, you will need some tools and inventory to get started so you should expect to invest in them—even in a legitimate network marketing company.
- *No unsold inventory buyback.* Legitimate network marketing companies will buy back unsold inventory for at least 70%-90% of what

> "... unlike pyramid or Ponzi schemes, MLMs have a real product to sell. More importantly, MLMs actually sell their product to members of the general public, without requiring these consumers to pay anything extra or to join the MLM system."
>
> —DEBRA A. VALENTINE, GENERAL COUNSEL, US FEDERAL TRADE COMMISSION[8]

NOTE:

MLM (Multi-Level Marketing) is another name for network marketing.

you paid. The guaranteed buyback is typically for at least a thirty-day period; some offer it for up to one year.

- *No focus on selling products or services, only on recruiting other distributors.*

Now you know more about the good and the bad news, as well as the advantages and disadvantages, of network marketing. You also better understand why legitimate network marketing companies are not pyramid or Ponzi schemes.

Bottom line: Legitimate network marketing companies pay compensation on both sales and signing up new distributors. It does not matter when you join; you can out earn your up-line. In Ponzi and pyramid schemes, on the other hand, the money goes to those at the top of the organization and pays out as new people are recruited, bringing with them a large investment. No products or services are sold. So if a company tells you that you do not have to sell any products or services to be paid a commission—step away.

Next, we'll look at the controls and restrictions that network marketing companies typically have.

Network Marketing Controls and Restrictions

Just like franchises, network marketing companies have controls and restrictions on how you are expected to conduct business. The intent is the same: to protect the value of their brand. While these controls may restrict what you really want to do—in order to make more sales and recruit more down-line distributors—they also make sure everyone is playing by the same rules.

1. **Restricted partnerships.** Some companies prevent you from working with another network marketing company even if the offerings do not compete. In this situation, if the company discovers your dual involvement, the company can terminate your distributorship. Your down-line would be moved to your former up-line and you would lose your commissions. On the other hand, some network marketing companies only restrict partnerships when products or services compete. It is not uncommon for someone in network marketing to be interested in representing several companies, so if this is your Plan B of choice, you will want to know your prospective companies' stance on this subject.

2. **Marketing and advertising.** You may be prevented from identifying the company or the product or service by name in your marketing. You may not be able to use their well-known logo in any advertising, and all you are left to work with is a description of benefits and features. The restrictions are in place so the company can ensure its logos and product or service descriptions are correctly and accurately used in what they deem an appropriate manner.

3. **Restricted Internet leverage.** Some companies do not allow you to advertise or sell its products or services on public websites such as eBay or Amazon. Although this is regularly violated, many network marketing companies have large legal staffs constantly searching for violators. Also, most companies have a system for distributors and others to report violations they notice, as a way to help keep the problem

to a minimum. In these situations, your ability to reach potential customers is limited to those you already know or can meet.

4. **Inventory.** Some product companies require you to purchase, store, and handle inventory, which increases your costs and decreases your profits. One former distributor told me she still has three $1,000 air filters sitting in her garage that she has never sold. And, just like with buying a business, if the inventory gets old, expires, or becomes dated, you will be stuck with unsellable products. Some companies, however, will drop ship the products directly to your customers, so delivery is automatically handled and you're required to take little or no action.

5. **Minimum purchase.** You may be required to make a minimum purchase of the products or services before receiving your first check from the company. You personally might have to make a monthly purchase of anywhere from a few dollars to over one hundred. Other companies only require an annual purchase of a few hundred dollars to remain an active distributor.

6. **Minimum volume.** As you become more successful, you will achieve higher pin titles with a larger percentage in commissions (as we discussed in the earlier *Advantages* section of this chapter). To maintain a pin title and commission percentage level, you may decide to buy more products yourself so you can achieve the minimum monthly volume requirement and remain at the same pin title and compensation level. Typically, you can miss the volume requirement one month and not lose your level; after that, any more missed months may result in you moving down a pin level and receiving a smaller percentage commission. This creates pressure to keep your sales volume up. But the same

thing happens in the other Plan Bs; you have to make sales to make money.

Network Marketing 101

The following illustrations show examples of products and services sold in network marketing companies and what percentage of the markets they hold.

Percent of Sales by Major Product Groups

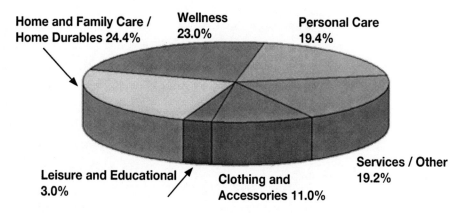

Home and Family Care / Home Durables 24.4%

Wellness 23.0%

Personal Care 19.4%

Services / Other 19.2%

Leisure and Educational 3.0%

Clothing and Accessories 11.0%

Home and Family Care/Home Durables: cleaning products, cookware, cutlery, candles, vacuum cleaners, air filters, and home appliances	24.4%
Wellness: weight loss products, vitamins, nutritional products, food, and beverages	23.0%
Personal Care: cosmetics, jewelry, skin care, and clothing	19.4%
Services/Other: legal, auto care, pet care, electric and natural gas in deregulated states, telephone services (local and long distance), satellite TV, home security, insurance, and financial products (e.g., mutual funds, insurance, variable annuities)	19.2%
Clothing and Accessories: men's, women's, children's, and pets'	11.0%
Leisure and Educational: books, videos, toys, and travel	3.0%

2010 Fact Sheet, Direct Selling Association (DSA), with additional category examples from Direct Selling News: 2010 DSN Global 100[9]

(This information is primarily from the Direct Selling Association, a national trade association of the leading firms that manufacture and distribute goods and services sold directly to consumers.)

Is Network Marketing the Best Plan B Option for Me?

We will soon apply the Six Key Ingredients and the Real Deal Checklist to help you evaluate network marketing companies.

Before we do that, however, there are a few more questions you should ask yourself if you're considering joining a network marketing company. These questions complement the work you did in chapters 2 and 5.

- Is this a product and/or service I love? You want offerings you would buy even if you weren't a distributor—offerings you would recommend without reservation to others.
- Do I feel I can sell or learn to sell this product or service? The core of making money in network marketing is sales to end users. So if you hate selling or are not willing to learn, this is not the Plan B option for you.
- Do I want to recruit, sponsor, and train others? The second part of network marketing is the ability sign up new distributors and help them become successful. You need to have the ability—or the desire to learn how—to attract, sponsor, and train your down-lines.
- Can I take rejection and keep going? Since you may have to recruit ten distributors just to find a top-selling one, you will spend a lot of time finding, re-

cruiting, and training new distributors who will, at some point, quit.

- Am I willing to work hard and not see much money for several years? Just like people in insurance sales, you may not see much money for the first three years or so of building your business. You will need staying power (and your powerful *why*) and to keep working toward your goal. All of the other Plan B options are like this too.

Keep reading if you feel comfortable with your answers to the questions above, and let's hone in on this Plan B!

Six Key Ingredients for Evaluating a Network Marketing Company

To illustrate the key ingredients, we'll use a variety of product and service offerings.

1. **Market trends in your favor.** Just like the growing trends discussed in the franchise chapter, networking marketing is impacted the same way. For example, the aging boomers have too much purchasing power to ignore, and they are interested in health and wellness, nutrition, and anti-aging products and services. So is the next-younger generation, Gen X, as they realize they will live a long time and want to do it while being active, healthy, and attractive. Diet products naturally remain steady and strong. There are increasing demands for all green products and pet offerings too.

> "Skin care, nutrition, and weight-management products will continue to drive the trends in the network marketing industry."
>
> —PAUL ZANE PILZER, AUTHOR, *THE NEXT MILLIONAIRES*

2. **Consumable products and ongoing services.** You want repeat customers. This is the single most important key ingredient for network marketing. You want to get customers hooked and to

sign them up to automatically renew the services or receive product shipments. This is what will eventually produce residual income for you for years to come. It's similar to what is called the razor blade model: Gillette literally gave away razors and made its money from selling the razor blades. Hewlett Packard (HP) sold low-cost printers and made its money from selling ink cartridges. Examples of consumable products are those in the skin care, cleaning, nutrition, vitamin, and cosmetic lines. Great examples of service offerings are in the areas of home security, long-distance telephone services, and electricity and natural gas in unregulated states. The faster your customers use up what you are offering, the better.

3. **Perfect timing.** Being ahead of the trends can be tough. You want to look for a network marketing company with a strong research-and-development focus and that is regularly launching new products or services to match the growing market trends that can be serviced by network marketing. Wellness and nutritional products are a growing trend that is a good match for network marketing. Services that help end users lower their satellite TV costs, for example, is another good match to a note-worthy trend. What you are really looking for is a company that has a history of offering products and services aimed at growing trends. Since it could take years to develop a single offering, the company must be future focused.

4. **Strong compensation or attractive margins.** This is probably the most complex and difficult part of network marketing—understanding how much money you will make. From a common sense prospective, if the products are priced low, you will

only make a little on each sale, so you'll have to make a lot more sales. Conversely, high-cost offerings will create bigger commissions, but each sale might be harder to make. It is the same for all of the Plan B options.

5. **Powerful partnerships.** There are four partnership areas to evaluate:

- The company (because this is part of determining how successful you will become over the long term)
- Its manufacturers or providers (you don't want to have your customers' trust shaken by a product recall or service failure)
- The partners the company collaborates with (you want the company to be working with organizations that are leaders in their industries)
- The experts that advise the company, such as an advisory board (again, you are looking for people who are recognized experts)

6. **Unique products or exclusive technology.** The more unique or exclusive the products and services, the better. As you already know, the most successful offerings eliminate a customer's pain or frustration, or provide pleasure. If the network marketing company is the only place to buy this particular product or service, you will make sales more easily. In the early days of Apple Computer, for example, the company's sales staff was described as order takers because the demand was so high for Apples. The company did it again with the iPhone and the iPad. So if you're a distributor for a company that has a unique product or exclusive technology, you'll make more money because the company can charge more for its offering. You don't want

consumers to be able to buy a substitute on eBay or Amazon.

Unfortunately, there is no disclosure document for network marketing companies like there is for franchises. Your due diligence, therefore, will take more effort. Most of your research will come from Internet searches and attending meetings and/or joining conference calls.

To evaluate a company, search for its name online and then:

- Read the company's press releases and, more importantly, what other neutral experts have to say.
- Look for awards, innovative offerings, and expert testimonials about sales growth (make sure the sales growth is from its products or services and not from signing more distributors).
- If the company is listed on a stock exchange, you will find more specific and accurate data than a company that isn't.
- Spend time on the company's website to see what is being bragged about. For some, it is only about sales. For others, it is about their partnerships and how they are helping their communities, for example.
- Research the executives by name and look for their business expertise, success, ethics, and values.
- Check with the Better Business Bureau (BBB) in the city and state of the network marketing company's headquarters for any unresolved complaints. But remember, you can expect to find a complaint filed against any company that is big and has been successfully in business for any length of time.
- If the company has events, such as a sales conference or monthly training sessions, attend them to see and

hear from the executives. Talk with them as well as the other attendees. Ask all of them how long they have been distributors and how much of a profit they make each month. This is very similar to conducting references with franchisees, as we covered in the previous chapter.

You can accurately evaluate companies by conducting your own research using the Six Key Ingredients list. You will quickly learn if the company is strong enough to continue to attract new customers and distributors. It will take some work, but you will want to do it because if the company goes out of business you will lose your commissions. This is the same as the other Plan B options and a Plan A job.

Use the Real Deal Checklist to Evaluate a Network Marketing Company

Let's use the Real Deal Checklist introduced to you in chapter 7 and apply it to two products from a network marketing company. Since baby boomers have such a huge purchasing potential, we will focus on two anti-aging products—a skin-care product and a nutritional supplement.

The skin-care product is a twice-a-day cleanser and moisturizer that has been scientifically verified to reduce fine lines and wrinkles with a skin punch biopsy (ouch!). The results are cumulative, so someone using the product look years younger.

The nutritional product is a daily capsule supplement that increases stamina (via more efficient energy production or the ability to convert calories to energy), increases a person's ability to concentrate, and improved sexual health

"I got into network marketing because I worked days and my husband worked nights; I was lonely. I love holding parties to help women look beautiful on the inside as well as the outside.

One of my tactics to motivate my unit is to send them cards weekly or monthly and let them know how much I appreciate them.

There have been times I made more in network marketing than I did in my Plan A job, and it only took three years of working part-time to get there."

—ROSE SAVOY,
FOURTEEN-YEAR
NETWORK MARKETER

resulting in increased sexual desire. It takes from a few days to two weeks to feel the stainable difference, which is significantly different than a high-caffeine or sugary energy drink that offers an immediate energy jump but that wears off in a few hours.

- *What:* The products have been developed and tested, and their claims have been scientifically confirmed by peer reviews and introduced at respected scientific conferences. The *range of applications* is straight forward: better-looking skin with the skin care product, increased stamina, concentration, and sexual health and desire through the nutritional product. The products are *practical* because most of us want to look better and feel better. Here's one reason why it is increasingly important: people stay in the workforce longer, which means that seasoned workers compete with new college graduates who have boundless stamina and no wrinkles. The need to look younger and have increased stamina has become critically important in the workplace. The *number of applications* is limited to skin care and nutrition. Both products are immediately *useable.* Since the company holds a number of patents on these products, there will be limited *competition* for the life of the patents. The results are visual because the skin-care results are *visible,* and the nutritional-supplement benefits can be felt.
- *Who:* Now let's identify the *target market.* The skin-care product will be of interest to those people who have or are starting to show lines and wrinkles—typically people start to see them in their mid- to late thirties. The skin-care market is specifically targeted to the seventy-

six million American boomers. The nutritional supplement's target market is also the boomers, plus athletes who want to increase their performance, and young mothers who feel exhausted from juggling many responsibilities. The *location* of the target market is across the United States and internationally. *Marketing and selling to reach* this target market is best achieved through personal contact (calling, e-mailing, having lunch), holding events (such as the parties Tupperware is famous for), and social media (e.g., Facebook). *How much* each customer will buy from you at one time and *how often* is pretty much fixed: the skin-care product is used twice daily and the nutritional supplement is taken once a day, which results in reordering on a regular basis. The company offers additional products that can accelerate the results of younger-looking skin and increased health with nutritional products. And perhaps most importantly, the *target market* is growing.

- *Why:* The *benefits* have already been identified—look better and feel better. The *pain* that will be eased or eliminated with the skin-care product is the embarrassment of looking old, with sagging skin and deep wrinkles. The nutritional supplement will help ease the frustration of those who feel exhausted all the time and are having a hard time focusing and concentrating. There will be *pleasure* for your customers when they know they look better and feel better. And we have already identified the *needs* that exist for looking better. The product or service *alternatives* for looking better include Botox treatments and plastic surgery. Botox treatments (these are shots!) last from three to four months. They have been developed from Botulinum toxin, and the injections cost from $500 to $1,500 per treatment. Plastic surgery costs are in the ten- to twenty-thousand-dollar-plus range. The *trends* related to skin care are the growing boomer population and the increasing pressure to look younger and fresher. The *trends* for the nutritional supplement are also tied to the aging boomer, plus the increasingly hectic lives so many of us lead, as well as the poor quality of the typical American diet.

- *How:* The network marketing company has already determined the best method to *fulfill* product orders. Although a distributor may maintain a small, personal inventory, the products are usually *warehoused* and then *shipped* by the company.

- *More:* The network marketing company may have other products or services you can offer to your customer at *higher prices,* but you can't create new ones. Like franchising, you're limited to what the company offers and by its restrictions and controls.

- *You:* You have already identified your areas of *expertise and strengths* and know what you have and which ones you are *missing.* A good approach is for a pair or a small number of distributors to create a partnership, thereby leveraging each other's strengths. For example, one person may be very good at recruiting but poor at closing the sale. Or one person is an excellent networker and gets people interested in the business but doesn't like to sponsor or train others. Another idea is to hire someone to assist you, such as a sales assistant who can set up appointments or make follow-up calls for you. This would be at your expense, of course.

The Two Methods to Make Sales in a Network Marketing Company

There are two ways to make sales in network marketing: *Bottom up,* which focuses on selling to the end users—your customers. *Top down,* which focuses on recruiting new distributors—your down-lines. Most successful distributors use both. Keep in mind some top-selling distributors have used primarily only one method and yet are making a high, six-figure annual income. Again, this goes back to you, your strengths, and what you are ready and willing to learn how to do.

First let's look at *where* and *how* network-marketing sales are made. This will determine the work lifestyle that will be needed to be successful. You have already identified the type you prefer in chapter 5.

You will see by the statistics on the next page face-to-face contact is the primary way that sales are made. The implications are that to be successful you will be doing most of your sales by holding meetings, doing presentations, and talking personally with others. Selling the products or services using the Internet is not as successful.

Let's continue to explore the two methods typically used to make sales, as well as the advantages and disadvantages of each.

Bottom-up sales focus on selling the products or services to the end user—your customers. The *advantage* of this method is you are building

How Network Marketing Sales are Typically Made
(Reported as a percentage of sales dollars)

Face-to-Face Selling
by Sellers
80.1%

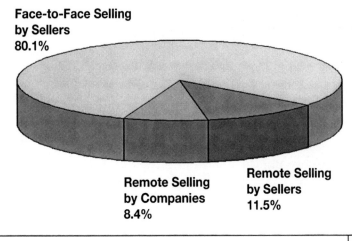

Remote Selling
by Companies
8.4%

Remote Selling
by Sellers
11.5%

Face-to-Face Selling by Sellers: home or office parties, one-on-one discussions, demonstrations, and trade shows	80.1%
Remote Selling by Sellers: telephone calls, Skype meetings, conference calls, and teleseminars. Also social media connections such as Facebook	11.5%
Remote Selling by Companies: website sales, and tradeshows	8.4%

2010 Fact Sheet, Direct Sales Association (DSA)[10]

monthly sales volume that ensures you maintain your pin title and commission percentages. With a steady and established automatic sales volume, you will not have to scramble at the end of the month to make enough sales to keep your commissions coming in.

One *disadvantage* is that you are the only salesperson, so your volume is limited to the sales you can personally make. Another disadvantage is that if your products or services don't have longevity or they are a me-too offering, you have a potentially high drop-out rate of customers and down-line distributors.

According to some trusted and top-selling distributors, the bottom-up approach is the best way for a newbie to start building a business. Once you have a stable number of customers and sales volume each month, you can start building your team using the top-down process.

Top-down sales focuses on recruiting new distributors to your business. Typically, they will also sell the products or services to their own end users. The *advantages* of top-down sales are that you get paid on the investment each new recruit makes *and* on their sales.

The *disadvantages* are that it takes time to recruit, train, and mentor your down-lines to become successful. Some recruits are fussy, sulky, or hard to coach. It takes time and energy to coach those who are difficult to work with. It is great fun to work with those that are energized, "get it," and are ready to go.

Many successful network marketers first build a stable platform of repeat customers (the bottom-up approach) and then recruit and train others to do the same (the top-down approach).

From your work in chapter 2, you may already know which of the two approaches is the most comfortable for you to begin to build your business. And remember, you can partner with someone who complements you, your skills, and your expertise.

Next, I will introduce you to two common network marketing compensation plans. It's simply an overview and is not meant to necessarily provide you with an in-depth understanding. Even though I worked with comprehensive, varied, and complex sales compensation plans in corporate America, I still found some of the network marketing company compensation plans confusing.

Typical Network Marketing Compensation Plans

This section is a brief introduction to two common types of compensation plans in network marketing companies.[11] Typically plans are complex and hard to understand. You may need to talk with the network marketing company's distributor support staff and have them show you how the compensation actually works before you commit to a particular network marketing opportunity. Your up-lines should know the compensation plan well, and will continue to educate you on how to keep track of the best ways to earn the highest commission each month. Since all Plan Bs are designed for you to make money, it's critical that you know how this works in the network marketing industry.

Before we launch into the descriptions, let's define a key term: Your *first level* refers to those distributors who sign up directly under you. They are your first level of down-lines. A significant part of your commission will be based on the sales of your down-lines. You may be paid on the sales of those just one level down or as many as six or more levels deep.

Network marketing compensation plans are designed to reward the few who work hard, are diligent, and have the traits needed to make the sales and to recruit others. Think of the 80/20 rule: only 20% do the work and will enjoy the highest financial rewards, just like the founders and executives of every other company.

There is a comprehensive description of four compensation plans (binary, stairstep breakaway, unilevel, and matrix) on the MLM Insider Online.[12] It will help you better understand how each plan works. It also provides you with the strengths and weaknesses, whether the plans are designed for either full-time or part-time workers and if they are geared toward personal consumption, retail sales, or both. And it has a list of which plans well-known companies are using. This site has the most easily understood and most comprehensive information I have been able to find.

Okay, back to the compensation plans. Let's take a brief look at two common types: *binary* and *breakaway*.

BINARY COMPENSATION PLAN

In a binary plan, your first level (the down-lines who sign up directly under you) is limited to two. As those two sign up other distributors under them, you will be paid on each distributor's sales for as deep as your team grows, which is referred to as *infinite depth*. You can only have two down-lines and each of them can only have two, and so forth. Thus, your business builds downward instead of building a wider group with a larger number of distributors directly under you.

STAIRSTEP BREAKAWAY COMPENSATION PLAN

> To be successful in network marketing will take what every other job does—hard work, focus, time, and follow through.
>
> But by picking the right company and up-line will make it easier.
>
> —KATHLEEN RICH-NEW, BUSINESS CONSULTANT, SPEAKER, EXECUTIVE COACH, CLARITY WORKS CONSULTING; AUTHOR, *PLAN B*

In a stairstep breakaway plan, you have an un-limited first level width of down-lines; you can sign up as many people as you want. Keep in mind you and your up-line will have to sponsor and train each of them, but then you will be paid on their volume of sales down several levels under you. The company usually offers you a *finite depth,* ranging from three to ten levels deep. The stairstep breakaway plan is the most commonly used compensation plan.

Due Diligence for Selecting a Network Marketing Company

Select a company you trust and have faith in its leaders—a company you can be proud of. Its leaders are your partners in product development, legal and financial issues, human resources, customer service, product development, order fulfillment, data processing, international expansion, public relations, ethics, and culture. The company's leaders are crucial to your long-term success, which is true for any organization.

What to look for in a company

1. **Minimum six years old.** The big money typically comes in year six or seven, and many new network marketing companies fail in their first five years. If you join a young company and build your team, and then the company fails, your income stops. But of course that is the same for all of the Plan B options—and your Plan A job. According to some estimates, thousands of network marketing companies have opened their doors since the 1950s; only about fifty companies made it to the ten-year mark and still remain in business today.

2. **At least $50 million in sales.** This shows the leaders have learned how to profitably provide the product or service, grow the company, and pay their bills. It also shows the company has appropriate elements of geometric progression, which is based on frequency, consistency, and time. This geometric progression—especially when combined with the company's earnings and the length of time the company has been in business—indicates the business is staged for significant growth in the next five years.

3. **Publicly traded.** If the company is traded on one of the stock exchanges, its finances are verifiable. If it is a private company, you will not have access to this information and will have to trust what they tell you. If the company is in trouble, the leaders may never tell you and you won't know until you read about it in the media. If the private company is more than ten years old, however, there may be less of a concern. You can also find out the company's Dun & Bradstreet and credit ratings to make sure it is in a solid financial state. As we noted earlier in this chapter, check with the Better Business Bureau in the headquarters' city and state for unresolved complaints.

4. **Verifiable science claims.** If there are science-based claims, ensure they are true. Science is based on measurement and therefore can be verified by peer-reviewed research findings presented at well-respected science conferences held around the world. Again, the Internet and the company website can help you. If the company's claims are based on anecdotal stories or a big-name celebrity, the company just wants you to trust them—which you shouldn't do. (For example, more than 1,500 supplement companies are all saying theirs is the

No. 1 supplement…so who is telling the truth?[13])
Many companies have famous celebrities or
athletes endorse their products, yet there are no
peer-validated clinical studies to back up their
claims. There is no science behind it.

5. **More than one offering.** It's best to have several options to offer customers. If you only have one product, then your success will have to be built on getting
new customers instead of selling more to the ones
you already have. There is also the danger of the offerings becoming outdated or duplicated.

6. **History of innovation.** If there are no new offerings, your only way to increase sales is to find new
customers.

7. **Consumable products.** The faster your end users
use up the products or services, the more sales you
make.

8. **Products are sole-source, patented, and exclusive.** Me-too products mean you are competing
with other network marketing companies or with
retail outlets that can offer them at the same or
lower prices.

9. **Multiple training ventures.** If you have not done
sales in the past, then training is very important.
You want the training opportunities to be available
at low or no cost. Some companies make a portion
of their profit from selling their distributor training.
With most companies, expect to have to personally
invest in additional sales training.

10. **Distributors have actually retired on residual
income.** Since one major reason to join a network
marketing company is residual income, you want
evidence that distributors have been successful. Ask
how many have retired on residual income from the
network marketing company. They may not be open
or willing to give this information to you, either be-

> "You will never
> be hurt by the
> opportunities you
> say no to. There's
> nothing wrong with
> patience. When a
> distributor tells you
> to get in now or
> you'll be sorry,
> don't get in."
>
> —JEFF PIERSALL,
> PRESIDENT AND
> COFOUNDER, SCB
> MEDIA; FORMER
> NETWORK MARKETING
> TOP-SELLING
> DISTRIBUTOR

cause they don't have the information, because no one has retired, or the successful distributors are having too much fun to retire.

11. **Does not compete with its distributors.** You want a company that makes decisions that support distributors. Apple Computer upset a lot of its retailers when it started selling computers directly to end users. Many of their retailers lost sales and some went out of business as a result.

12. **A growing demographic of end users.** You want your end user base to be growing, not shrinking. With aging baby boomers making up a third of the world population and controlling 50% of the wealth in the United States, anything that appeals to them will automatically give you a growing customer base. Consider the market trends from the chapter on franchises to help you identify potential demographic bases.

13. **Little or no inventory requirements.** You don't want to tie up your money or your garage with a lot of inventory. Also, remember that if you have to buy the products and then sort and deliver them, you are using a lot of time doing routine work that does not grow your business. So a company that drop ships the products to customers frees you to focus on finding new customers and down-lines.

14. **Products are guaranteed.** Offerings should have a money-back guarantee with a no-questions-asked policy. If the company can't offer at least a thirty-day, money-back guarantee, then they don't believe in their own offerings. Also, if it's a lot of hassle to return the product or get a refund on the service, your customers will rarely buy from you again.

15. **Leaders, founders, and corporate executives.** "Leadership may not be the only thing that makes

companies successful but it is pretty close," is what I frequently tell others. Do your research to ensure the leaders are honest, ethical, have high morals and values, and are financially conservative. Internet searches are quick and easy. Remember, the company's leadership determines the future of the organization's success or downfall. If you are building your future on residual income, you want to make sure it will be there for you. Certainly the greed that permeated worldwide financial scandals in the past decade came from the decisions the leaders made that benefited only themselves.

16. **Member of the Direct Selling Association (DSA).** Company members of the DSA are committed to higher standards and ethics. The DSA has approximately two hundred members, so using this as a criterion can automatically narrow the number of companies you consider. However there are high-quality network marketing companies that are not members, so just use the list as a guide.

17. **Transferrable and sellable.** Since you would have spent years building a successful team (your organization) you want the same options you have for the other Plan B businesses—to either sell it or have your family inherit it. There will be specific terms and conditions for each option that will have to be met that the company's legal department can provide.

This list of seventeen items will help you choose a successful company. You want any company you are considering to match at least seven of the criteria from the list. Look at trade-offs too. For example, if a company is not traded on the stock market but it has been in business and growing for at least ten years and has an excellent credit rating, then that useful information can be an acceptable trade-off for not being publicly traded. Or if the company's distributor training is one of its profit centers, but the majority of the company's earnings is from its offerings, this can be okay too. You will need to decide which factors are the most important for you.

Selecting Your Up-Line

After you have found a good company, your next important decision is to find the best up-line to sponsor and mentor you. That is a lot easier said than done because you won't be able to get a list of top-performing distributors from the company. One way to find up-lines you want to work with is to attend meetings and/or training events in your area so you can meet these stellar sellers. Begin your due diligence to learn more about them and their up-lines. You may also have the opportunity to meet some of their cross-lines that you may find to be a better fit for you. Be forewarned, as soon as you attend a meeting to learn more about the business, you may find yourself surrounded by distributors who want to recruit you. Most network marketing companies have a strictly hands-off policy for a week or two after the event unless you proactively contact another distributor who may seem to be a better fit for you.

There is a commonly mistaken expectation that you are obligated to sign up with the first person who talks to you about the network marketing company. You are not! You need to sign up with someone you feel you can trust, and someone who can help you become successful. In network marketing companies, just like in any business enterprise, there are obnoxious, ego-centered people who only care about the sales you make. I have sat in on enough training calls to know there are top-selling

> There is a commonly mistaken expectation you are obligated to sign up with the first person who talks to you about the network marketing company. You are not!
>
> —KATHLEEN RICH-NEW, BUSINESS CONSULTANT, SPEAKER, EXECUTIVE COACH, CLARITY WORKS CONSULTING; AUTHOR, *PLAN B*

distributors who approach their business and down-lines as strict, critical, and demanding parents who scream and brag how they didn't take a day off for three years and had to miss anniversaries, family birthdays, and children's events. I have also been on calls with top sellers who are fun, nurturing, and caring. Choose your up-line wisely, and do *not* feel any obligation to sign up with the first person you speak with.

Once you find a few potentially excellent up-line distributors, do your research on them too. Google their names. If the word *Scam* shows up next to a name, proceed slowly and very cautiously, if you proceed at all.

If you are approached by someone you don't know and who wants you on his or her network marketing team, use the up-line Due Diligence Checklist below to help you determine if the person is a good match for you.

Up-Line Due Diligence Checklist

1. **Successful in another industry.** The same skills it takes to succeed in most businesses are required in network marketing.
2. **Successful in network marketing.** If the one recruiting you is fairly new to the business, find a knowledgeable and experienced person above him or her. Like new mountain climbers who use guides to help them, you need people who have already climbed the mountain. They can tell you where the best paths and handholds are to reach the top. Since only a small percentage will succeed, you want to stack the deck in your favor.
3. **A long-term commitment to the team and business.** Your direct up-line should have been in the business long enough for the honeymoon-type of

emotions to cool and to have made the emotional switch from novelty to commitment.

4. **Respected and respectful.** There are a lot of arrogant, temperamental, pushy network marketing distributors trying to recruit people like you. You want to be able to go to your up-line for help and to expect their support. If you feel intimidated or they act annoyed, you will avoid them and eventually quit.

5. **Caring.** You want someone who goes slow enough to learn about your wants and your concerns, yet can keep pace with you when you're ready to forge ahead. Listen closely to determine if this person's suggestions support you.

6. **Trust.** Look for people who are dedicated, loyal, focused, positive, committed, generous, and successful. Use your gut and your ears. Their actions need to match their words. You want them to tell you what you need to hear, instead of what you *want* to hear. If you are uncomfortable, keep looking.

7. **Helpful.** Do they have the time, knowledge, skills, and ability to help you?

Keep in mind that there are new distributors whose up-line disappeared on them for whatever reason, and yet they still figured out the business on their own and built a successful team. So even though I am suggesting you find an up-line that is a good match for you, some distributors are successful with or without one.

Network marketing typically requires a three- to five-year plan to build your business. It is sales—not a rocket ship—and it will take time to build your customer base and your team. There is a lot to learn, so don't quit your Plan A day job to join a network marketing company. If you are employed, stay there until you are making twice your salary for at least three years in a row. For example, if you are making $50,000 a year at your day job, stay there until you have made $100,000 from network marketing for three consecutive years. This advice came from several of the top-performing network marketing distributors I talked with.

Yes, you can earn a profit the first month and many people do. Some people will earn an extra $500 a month; a smaller number of people who are willing to learn, who are coachable, and who work hard will earn $3,000 or more each month. The top 1% of earners can reach more than $500,000 a year. But all of it will take the skills and ability to build a stable team of distributors and loyal customers, as well as the willingness to stay focused and do the work. This is the same requirement for any type of success in life.

Wrap Up

You now have a deeper understanding of network marketing than most of the people working in the industry. You learned the good and bad news as well as the advantages and disadvantages. We also clarified the confusion some people have about the network marketing industry itself.

> "Your success is hidden in your daily routine of self discipline by managing your time and priorities."
>
> —JOE PICI. CO-FOUNDER AND COO, PICI AND PICI, AUTHOR, SELL NAKED ON THE PHONE AND SALES TRAINING5

You know the most common types of products and services sold and how to select a network marketing company. We applied the Six Key Ingredients and the Real Deal Checklist to two different products: a skin care product and a nutritional supplement. You examined the two methods for making sales in network marketing, and we looked at two common compensation plans and how to conduct your own due diligence on companies and your prospective up-line.

The next and final chapter shows you how to put your Plan B into action. We'll start by briefly reviewing the first ten chapters and showing you several inspiring Plan B success stories. You will also learn how to narrow your Plan B options using your work from chapter 2 on determining your *why*. Last but not least, you will use your work from chapter 5 to determine where the time and money will come from, how to achieve the work lifestyle you desire, and how to draft your exit plan.

Turn the page and get ready to determine your best Plan B option, and to learn what you need to do next.

You have done the hard work, and now it's time to fly!

Notes

1   "Global Statistical Report, 2010"
     World Federation of Direct Selling Associates,
     http://www.wfdsa.org/files/pdf/global-stats/
     Global_Statistical_Report_11311.pdf
2   "The Top 25 Network Marketing Companies"
     Nexera LLC
     www.nexera.com/top25/
3   "2010 Fact Sheet"
     Direct Selling Association,
     http://www.dsa.org/research/industry-statistics/
4   Nexera, "Top 25"
5   Joe Pici
     Cofounder and COO, Pici and Pici, Inc.
     author
     Sell Naked On the Phone, Sales Training
     www.PiciandPici.com
6   "Network Marketing, Ponzi scheme, Pyramid
     scheme"
     Wikipedia, accessed December 2011
     www.wikipedia.org

7   Ibid

8   Debra A. Valentine
    general counsel, US Federal Trade Commission
    from a prepared statement on pyramid schemes
    May 13, 1998
    http://www.ftc.gov/speeches/other/dvimf16.shtm

9   "2010 Fact Sheet" DSA
    see also *Direct Selling News: 2010 DSN Global 100*
    for additional category examples:
    http://directsellingnews.com/index.php/view/
    dsn global 100 the top selling companies in the
    world

10 "Location of Sales (reported as a percentage of
    sales dollars)" table "2010 Fact Sheet," DSA
    http://www.dsa.org./research/industry-
    statistics/#PRODUCT

11 Glenn Brooks
    "Network Marketing—MLM compensation plans"
    Network Marketing-Works!
    www.network marketing-works.com/compensationplans.
    htm accessed 2010
    Glenn Brooks is an Internet and network marketing
    trainer.

12 "MLM Insider Compensations Plans Explained"
    MLM Insider Online
    http://mlminsider.com/main.php?/compensation
    plans

13 John Whitaker
    Network Marketing presentation
    Melbourne Beach, FL, 2010
    John is a retired military officer, corporate executive,
    and a top-selling network marketing distributor. He
    also earned degrees in chemistry and biology and is
    a former nutrition-store owner.

CHAPTER 11

Putting Your Plan B into Action

CONGRATULATIONS! You are now ready for your Plan B's next logical step.

If you already know exactly what your Plan B will look like, that's great, but if you haven't decided on a path or a plan, don't worry. There is a lot to learn about the various Plan B options, but I can assure you that you are further along than you think.

Let's take a few minutes to review how much work you have already done and to appreciate how much you have learned.

- Chapter 1, "I Worked Hard, I Played by the Rules, *and This Is All I Get?*" was designed to help those of you who had already realized you need a Plan B but didn't know what to do about creating one. This first chapter also reassured you that you are not alone. For readers who felt secure in their Plan A jobs and didn't think they needed a Plan B, this chapter hopefully served as a wake-up call. These are our most vulnerable readers because their jobs and careers may be moving offshore and not coming back. Or their pension is suddenly reduced or disappears completely. Or an employer downsizes and employees are laid off.

- Chapter 2, "Is Your *WHY* Bigger than Your *BUT?*" helped you identify your powerful why for a Plan B, the life values you are currently most dissatisfied with, and what you don't and do want in your future. This defining work has and will continue to help you identify the future you are ready to create.

- Chapter 3, "The Real Deal about You," introduced the hero's journey, which you might very well experience in the near future. Holly Wilder shared her hero's journey with us as she built her cupcake empire. You also learned the key traits of serial entrepreneurs and what they most value. The five requirements for successful change were spelled out so you know what you must have to create the changes in your life and develop a Plan B. I also encouraged you to listen carefully to the right people.

- Chapter 4, "There Are Many Paths to a Plan B," gave you the packing list for your future, including the importance of your *why*, the type of mindset you'll need, how to identify the right opportunity and the right timing and the new skills best suited to your Plan B, and the importance of choosing a proven training program and the right team. You were introduced to the four Plan B options, and you learned how the Wealthy 1% of the US population has made its money.

- Chapter 5, "Thinking It Through: Avoiding the Pitfalls of Wrong (and Costly) Decisions," helped you identify where to find the resources to create your Plan B. You decided what work lifestyle you prefer by identifying your preferred work location and your workday's characteristics. You determined the energy and stamina that will be physically and mentally required from you, what the emotional toll may be for you, and your exit strategy.

- Chapter 6, "Six Key Ingredients of the Most Successful Companies," introduced you to what successful businesses have in common. We introduced you to the Six Key Ingredients that we later applied to each of the four Plan B options. You also learned some universal truths for business, such as *Nothing happens until someone sells something, You will have to become someone bigger and better,* and *Nothing is ever an overnight success.*

- Chapter 7, "The Real Deal about Starting Your Own Business," introduced you to the first Plan B option and provided you with the good and bad news and the advantages and disadvantages of a business start-up. You learned there are two types of start-ups— duplication and innovation. You were also introduced to the Real Deal Checklist, which we used to help new business owner Kate see all of the product and service possibilities her consulting practice can offer companies to manage project implementations more efficiently and effectively.

- Chapter 8, "The Real Deal about Buying a Business," introduced the second Plan B option and gave you its good and bad news as well as its advantages and disadvantages. We applied the Six Key Ingredients and the Real Deal Checklist to see what Paul, a young professional who was buying a tanning salon business, should have seen. You learned how to begin your search to find a business to buy, and the role business brokers can play to help you find a good business. You also learned how to conduct your own due diligence by using a company's business listing information and the selling memorandum. You learned the steps involved in buying a business so you will know what to expect during the process.

- Chapter 9, "The Real Deal about Buying a Franchise," is the third Plan B option. Here, you learned the good and bad news about the franchise industry. You also learned about its advantages and disadvantages, as well as the controls and restrictions that franchisors typically impose on their franchisees. You read the questions to ask yourself (which complement the work you already did in chapters 2 and 5) about franchising in general, as a way to determine if buying a franchise is a good fit and, if so, which types of franchises will work best for you. The Six Key Ingredients and the Real Deal Checklist were applied to several different types of franchises. The four franchise models were explained. You learned how to find a good franchise by yourself, as well as the role a broker plays in selling a franchise and what are the advantages and disadvantages of using a broker. You also learned the questions to ask when evaluating brokers. You learned that a franchise advisor, on the other hand, is an industry expert you can hire to work for you and thus make a better buying decision. You learned how to conduct your own due diligence by using the government-mandated Franchise Disclosure Document (FDD) and to consider whether you want to buy a new or an existing franchise. You also learned which areas of the franchise industry are growing.

- Chapter 10, "The Real Deal about Network Marketing," is the fourth of the four Plan B options. Naturally, we covered the good and bad news about the network marketing industry, as well as the advantages and disadvantages. This chapter addressed the confusion some people have about legitimate network marketing companies versus Ponzi and pyramid schemes. You learned about the typical controls and restrictions network marketing companies impose, the most common types of products and services sold, and the size of each of the categories. We applied the Six Key Ingredients and the Real Deal Checklist to two typical offerings. You read more questions to ask yourself to select the type of company you would be most interested in. Next, you learned the two ways that network marketing teams are built and the recommended way to start yours. You also learned such facts as 80% of network marketing sales are made face to face and only 11% by telephone. You received a brief overview of two common compensation plans, and you have hopefully realized that most of them will be hard to understand. You also learned how to conduct your own due diligence on network marketing companies. Lastly, you learned how to select the person or people you will work with, i.e., your up-line, and how to conduct due diligence on them.

Put your hands together and applaud yourself! Hurray for you!

Now, look at everything you have learned. You have worked hard, you were diligent, and here you are in the last chapter. You have probably learned more than you realize. If this were a master's level college curriculum (and it probably should be), you would be almost ready to graduate with your master of business administration degree in "Plan B" (we could call it an MPB instead of an MBA). In the space of these pages, you have learned what probably 80% of those currently working on or in a Plan B don't know. Most importantly, you know the good, the bad, and the ugly about each of the Plan B options and how to apply this information to your own Plan B's development.

Your work in this book will dramatically increase your chances of success because you have been willing to ask yourself the hard questions that others did not want to know or did not know even to ask. You've realized the importance of being clear about the decisions you make because you could find yourself working in your Plan B for the next five to ten years or longer.

As I said in the introduction, my undergraduate and two master's degrees in business did not teach me the information you have just learned. I became an *accidental* Plan B expert by researching each of the options as I tried to find one that suited me. It took a lot of digging, interviewing, and reading to be able to give you the good and bad news about each Plan B option, and the advantages and disadvantages too. Part of my own frustration was that almost everyone wanted to talk about only the good news of whatever they were selling, and the advantages of whatever path they'd chosen. It took a lot more time and effort to find out the bad news and the harsh reality of the disadvantages. Yet without this balanced view, none of us can make the best decision.

As you know, I have made several costly mistakes, primarily because I did not have the information this book provides. I jumped too fast and did not have a good grasp of the time and money my plan required. And I had not yet identified the Six Key Ingredients or developed the Real Deal Checklist, which are now key concepts in my speaking and teaching events.

Once you decide on a Plan B option, get started on it right away because it will take time to create it. Consider Thomas Edison's response to a reporter who asked how it felt to fail two thousand times before creating a successful light bulb. Edison's answer: "I never failed once. It just happened to be a two-thousand-step process." He reminds us we can expect to be on a journey that may take us down a variety of paths before we achieve success. Few people will find their answers because of going in a straight line, but most people will find their answers if they just *keep* going.

Take time to celebrate both your successes and your failures. For example, let's say you're working at a franchise for a few weeks as part of your research, and you realize that you hate like it. Wonderful! You have just saved yourself thousands or even millions of dollars, years of frustration, and the pain of what it would have taken to break the franchisor's ten-year contract. Or you may find you like the freedom that network marketing gives you once you have learned how to sell the products or services. Celebrate everything you've learned!

So what do I recommend as the best mindset for your journey? To enjoy the ride!

Plan B Success Stories

As you learned in chapter 2, the answer to success in each of the Plan B options is to ease or eliminate pain or to bring pleasure now or in the future.

Each of the business founders described next knew what they could offer the world…and they became multi-millionaires. As you read these success stories, apply what

you have learned so you can see what these business owners had in common and why their businesses flourished[1]:

- Brian Scudamore, founder of 1-800-GOT JUNK,
  started by knocking on doors and offering to haul
  away junk in his pickup truck for a fee. At first, he
  thought of helping people get rid of the junk sitting in their backyards and garages as a way to make
  some pocket money. Eventually, it developed into a
  full-time business with shiny trucks, a certain level
  of professionalism, and top-notch customer service.
  It then became the nation's largest junk-removal service. Brian saw the pain that junk created, and he
  literally removed the problem.

- Brian Taylor created Kernel Season's Popcorn Seasonings to make his own nightly popcorn snack
  tastier. He was a philosophy major at the University of Michigan when he started experimenting
  with the seasonings. Brian used $7,000 he had
  saved from working summer jobs to create a line
  of flavors and to set up a website. He convinced
  the owner of a local movie theater to try some, and
  the next week another movie theater owner called
  and wanted to try some too. Annual sales are now
  over $6 million. Brian brought pleasure to popcorn
  enthusiasts.

- Sheri Schmelzer, a stay-at-home mom, tried to
  keep her three young daughters entertained, so she
  pulled out their arts and crafts and sewing kits and
  then attached tiny silk flowers in the holes of their
  Crocs shoes. Husband Rich understood the business side of it when he saw the girls' delight as they
  showed him their newly decorated shoes. He applied
  for a patent with the brand name Jibbitz. The girls
  soon touted their shoe decorations to friends, and
  Jibbitz has now made them multi-millionaires. Sheri

brought fun and pleasure to her daughters, their friends, and millions of other girls.

• Joseph Semprevivo was diagnosed with diabetes at age nine. His parents created a great-tasting sugar-free cookie to satisfy his sweet tooth. Joseph's Lite Cookies also found an even bigger audience with people watching their weight. The company now offers sugar-free cookies, as well as fat-free cookies, brownies, cakes, and syrups. The products not only bring the pleasure of a healthier alternative to consumers, but they also reduce the pain of diabetics and weight watchers who aren't able to enjoy traditional sweets.

All these companies were started on a part-time basis and evolved as the business idea became successful.

The above examples describe business start-ups, because this Plan B option has more specific information *publicly* available than do the other Plan B paths. I know from working with my clients, however, that there are many similar stories for each of the other Plan B paths, but unfortunately I'm not at liberty to publicly share them.

Get Busy Narrowing Your Options

If you haven't done it already, it's now time to determine which Plan B option or options are the best match for you.

You have probably already eliminated one or two of them. But for each option you are considering, you will want to further evaluate them. You'll do this by making a chart for each option, and then hanging the charts next to each other or putting them on opposite walls or even

> If you are focused only on money and not on your passion, or on what you want in your life, or on helping others, then you probably won't succeed. You need more for your *why* than the desire to acquire money if you're going to handle the ups and downs of a Plan B.
>
> —KATHLEEN RICH-NEW, BUSINESS CONSULTANT, SPEAKER, EXECUTIVE COACH, CLARITY WORKS CONSULTING; AUTHOR, *PLAN B*

in different rooms. You decide what will work best for your decision-making process.

Here are the steps:

1. **Create a chart.** Get posterboard or a sheet of flip-chart paper and hang it on a wall or a door. At the top of each chart, put a summary of what you have decided you want in your Plan B (your work from chapters 2 and 5). Make it as long or short as you like. Write the Plan B option you are considering underneath your summary.

2. **Divide the chart in half.** Label one side *PRO* and the other side *CON*. List what you feel are the advantages (the pros) and disadvantages (the cons). I've listed below some topics to help get you started. Use your summary as a guide to determine if your ideas are moving you toward (pro) or away from (con) what you want. Consider using color-coded Post-it Notes—yellow for the cons and green or blue for the pros.

If you need help getting started on your pros and cons, use *Money, Time,* and *Work Lifestyle* for your first three topics or categories. Here are several questions you can use to develop your pros and cons:

- *Money:* How will your sales be made? How much money will it take to get started and to pay the bills until you are making a profit? How much money do you have or can get access to? What are your profit expectations? Whatever your cost estimate is, increase it by 50% because plans rarely go as smoothly as expected. Reminder: you have already answered some of these questions in chapter 5.

- *Time:* How much time will your Plan B option require to get started? How long until you decide to exit it? How much time do you have to dedicate to it? How long will it take you make a profit? As with your money estimate, increase the amount of time it will take by 50%. Sometimes things come up that will distract you, or there may be problems you had not anticipated. For example, the highly popular and successful Southwest Airlines early on battled a lawsuit filed by other airline companies trying to keep Southwest from flying. It took Southwest four and a half years to finally take its first flight. Stuff happens. Again, you identified some of your answers in chapter 5.

- *Work Lifestyle:* How closely does this Plan B option match the work lifestyle and the life values you identified in your answers in chapter 2? What are the hours you will be working? Where will you work from? Is it the type of work you like and want to do? Will you enjoy the type of people who will be your customers? Will the work energize or drain you? Will it be fun or hard? Some of your answers are in chapter 2.

On the next page is an example of what your chart might look like. You'll likely complete your chart in a few hours because you have already done most of the work.

3. **Once you have finished, step back and see what your chart is telling you.** Is the pro side filled with a lot of big advantages, and the con side has only a few notes that you can overcome? Or did you eliminate the option after covering these first three topics?

Plan B Option You are Evaluating

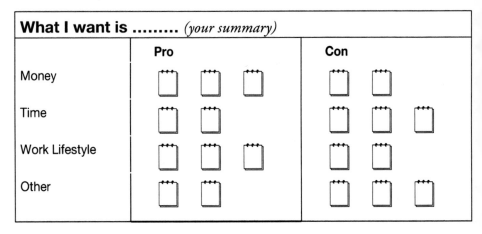

This chart will provide you with the answers that can help you get to a *no* faster. You want to get to *no* as fast as you can so you don't waste time researching and working on something that you will not or can not pursue.

You see how this process can help you decide which Plan B options are the best match for you.

Researching Your Chosen Plan B Option

Now that you have narrowed your options, it is time to begin implementing one.

No matter which path you choose, start by reviewing the chapter on that particular Plan B path. Spend more time applying the Six Key Ingredients from chapter 6 and working with the Real Deal Checklist from chapter 7 to your chosen path, especially now that you've studied the pros and cons of at least one potential path.

Please keep in mind that while this book will help you decide which Plan B is your best option, it does not have all of the answers. It is simply designed to get you started. For example, we have not addressed such topics as the various legal permits or licenses you may need, property or health insurance, taxes, or how to find funding or investors.

Thus, you will want to use additional resources. To help you out, each of the upcoming sections lists other resources.

No matter which Plan B option you select, it will require work, diligence, and focus. Expect it to take at least a year and more likely an average of three years before you make a profit. Even if you are buying an existing, profitable company, there will be much to learn to keep it profitable.

Starting a Business

If you choose this path, start by working through the Six Key Ingredients and the Real Deal Checklist. After that, you may also want to use one of SCORE's expert business consultants to review your plan. SCORE (www. SCORE.org) provides free online and face-to-face business counseling, mentoring, training, business templates, assessments, podcasts, and advice for small businesses just starting out or hoping to expand. The Small Business Administration (SBA) offers similar resources, so plan to spend time on both websites and/ or talking with their experts. Visit the SBA at www.SBA.gov.

Your community may also have a Small Business Development Center (SBDC) that is associated with the SBA, and it may have experts to help you. Visit http://www.sba.gov/content/small-business-development-centers-sbdcs. Also look for other entrepreneur centers that offer classes, usually at a low cost. Examples of classes you can expect to find: how to write business plans; basic marketing; customer service; and accounting. Some colleges offer studies in entrepreneurialism via courses on campus or online. The Kauffman Foundation (www.kauffman.org) is well known for advancing education and training in entrepreneurialism.

If you don't fully understand what it takes to start and run a small business, you may want to consider working at least part-time in one with an owner who will mentor you. Your goal would be to understand the dynamics of what it will actually take to run a small business on a daily basis. For example, if you want to start a restaurant, work part-time in one. Or if you want to start a computer-repair service, get yourself hired at one. Also, the *For Dummies* book series (www.Dummies.com) usually has helpful information on a variety of topics.

Buying a Business

Chapter 8 showed you how to start your search for a business by using the Internet and the MLS websites that list multiple companies that are for sale. You will find a variety of business listings in various geographic locations when you search the Internet for "business for sale" websites.

Start familiarizing yourself with what is actively available in your community or in the industry that is of interest to you. Be sure to use the Six Key Ingredients and the Real Deal Checklist to analyze each business you scrutinize.

If you decide to buy an existing business, seriously consider using two or three business brokers to help in your search. You've already learned that someone with a Certified Business Intermediary (CBI) has at least three years' experience and has undergone seventy hours of curriculum and rigorous testing. (To learn more about CBIs, visit www.ibba.org and click on the link for "Become a CBI" under the Brokers tab.) A CBI may offer better advice than someone without the certification. However, since less than 5% of business brokers are certified, you also have a list of questions to evaluate the other 95%.

Between 80% and 90% of the work involved with buying a business is the due diligence on the financial section of the Confidential Business Review. Be sure to require the current owner prove the accuracy of every claim he or she has made about the business. Bankers can also be of help here; they don't take at face value what anyone says, and you can use this to your advantage.

Buying a Franchise

Buying a franchise is also called buying a business-in-a-box because the business model has been developed, tested, and duplicated. Once you know this is the path you want, you can go shopping at a franchise exposition and/or find franchise brokers or advisors. Since franchise *brokers* are paid commission by the franchisors, they will only offer you the companies they work with. Or you can hire a franchise *advisor* to work for you to find good franchisors and to steer you away from the not-so-good ones. Use the questions in chapter 9 to evaluate brokers and advisors.

Review the advantages and disadvantages of the franchise model. Evaluate any franchise using the Six Key Ingredients and the Real Deal Checklist. Remember: the good franchisors have shown they are long-term players in the marketplace, they are profitable, and they make decisions in support of their franchisees.

There are a number of franchise associations with buyer's guides and frequently asked questions on their websites. There are also events at which you can shop for a variety of franchises at one time. Be sure to interview current franchise owners as well as previous owners who have left the company. You want as clear of a picture as possible of what you can expect from the franchisor and the company.

Internet ad portals can also direct you to various franchises. Popular portals include www.FranchiseGator.com, www.Franchise Solutions.com, www.FranchiseDirect.com, www.Franchising.com, www.BizBuySell.com, and www.Entrepreneur.com.

Network Marketing

If network marketing is your choice, chapter 10 has examples of the types of products and services that are typically sold by network marketing companies and the approximate size of each of the categories. The Direct Selling Association (www.DSA.org) lists its members and their contact information on its website. This can help you narrow the number of companies to consider from thousands to a few hundred. However, there may be good network marketing companies who are not members, so the DSA membership list is only one criteria to use in your decision-making process. Use the due diligence tasks in chapter 10 to further evaluate potential companies. Of course, you will also want to evaluate the companies using the Six Key Ingredients and the Real Deal Checklist.

Network marketing is arguably the simplest Plan B option because your roles are only to sell the products and/or services and to recruit other distributors to do the same. This path is also the least expensive in the beginning, with an initial investment ranging from a few hundred to a little over a thousand dollars. Since all of the Plan B options require the ability to make sales, this may be the best option for you to start building your business skills—especially managing your time and priorities—because these are so critical to successful sales. The mistake most people make when they get in to network marketing is that they do so for emotional reasons that they don't or can't convert to commitment to do the hard work.

Veterans, Active Military, and Trailing Spouses

If you have been or are in the military, there are special government-funded programs and resources available to you. Since these programs change and can be complex to understand, contact the SBA (www.sba.gov), the US Department of Veterans Affairs (www.va.gov), or Veterans' Business Outreach Centers (www.vboc.org) to learn more about the government programs. There may also be special Plan B-type support that will be of assistance for trailing spouses.

Wrap Up

You now know how to put your Plan B in action. You've reviewed what you learned in the first 10 chapters, and you have read several inspirational Plan B success stories. You also know that all successes take time to achieve. You narrowed your Plan B options to a manageable few, based on such criteria as the time you have and will need to get the business started, the amount of money you have and will need to invest, and how well an option matches your desired work lifestyle.

Wow, what a journey you have been on! You are amazing. Stand up and stomp your feet and slap yourself on the back. You deserve it!

So now you see that there are always options, whether you are a bone-weary road warrior who wants to get off the corporate treadmill, or a laid-off worker, or a retiree who is forced to return to work. In every economy, someone is making money and growing a business—you can too.

It is more possible than ever to create a Plan B today. And what you have learned in this book makes it even easier.

The economy is tough and unlikely to change anytime soon. Now, more than ever, everyone needs a Plan B.

Keep reading to learn how Plan Bs are helping more people and organizations.

The Increasing Popularity of a Plan B

The idea of a Plan B is taking on a life of its own. From companies creating Plan B work groups to me leading Plan B workshops or speaking at conferences and events, people are waking up to possibilities they did not see before.

Many people are realizing for the first time that they can take control of their life. Even if taking control means deciding to stay focused on a Plan A job for as long as it's available, people now know they have options.

Let's look at how *Plan B* can and is helping many people and organizations:

• *Companies* faced with unavoidable layoffs are offering their loyal employees more help than just classes on how to write a résumé and improve their interviewing skills. Since these employees will likely find jobs scarce and age discrimination alive and well, they're benefitting from learning about a Plan B.

- *Government organizations* such as the Workforce Development Boards and unemployment agencies are giving clients the real deal on the Plan B options those clients are considering. This means these organizations are helping their clients quickly evaluate an idea's potential and its possible success or failure. It also means people can get back to work faster.
- *Chambers of commerce* are using this book and the Plan B program to add value for their new members, many of whom have only held a job in the past and don't have a strong understanding of business basics. Other chamber members see how to become more profitable by expanding their products and services and finding new customers.
- *Lending institutions* use this information to more quickly educate their borrowers on how to start a new business or make a current one more profitable and successful.
- *Franchise companies* use this Plan B information to help prospective franchisees better understand the industry and what it takes to succeed. Better-educated franchisees enjoy a higher rate of success, and franchisors spend less time answering basic questions.
- *Network marketing companies* find it easier to talk with potential distributors when those newbies have learned what it takes to find a good company and up-line. By learning more about the Plan B concept, potential distributors understand in advance what they will need to do to be successful. As a result, companies have fewer distributors drop out. (The *really* good companies and up-lines give this book to those prospects they are recruiting.)
- *Parents of children who have high school or college diplomas* but can't get jobs are realizing how much this

book helps young people start to see and create their future.

As you know, my mission is to help people take control of their life so they wake up excited about work instead of dreading the day that lies ahead. I am elated and over-joyed every time the light bulbs click on when I speak at events and the attendees start thinking about how they really can create a successful Plan B—and change their lives.

Being on purpose and staying focused on your goals and desires is a process. It is a learned strategy and does not come naturally. We can symbolically walk together hand in hand so you can create what you want.

Plan B has been the roadmap to financial independence and a sense of fulfillment for so many. I would love to add your journey to my success stories.

Let me know how this book has helped you. Contact me at Kathleen@PlanBCoach.com.

My love and prayers are with you on your Plan B adventure,

Kathleen

Notes

1. How I Made My Millions, CNBC
www.cnbc.com

Appreciation and Acknowledgements

There is always a back story to any successful venture and a major part of that back story is the people who have helped create it. I have been blessed to have received incredible help from:

- Experts who freely shared their knowledge and advice and let me quote them.
- My students who joined me in my first Plan B seminar as I was still testing my ideas and materials. And those students who volunteered to review the first very, very rough draft of this book providing me with more feedback and suggestions.
- My book coaches who helped me find the right message and make the information more usable. Jan King was the first one who helped me explore the author's world.
- The radio and television producers and print editors who told me to send them the book when I finish it. They gave me the confidence to decide to write Plan B.
- My editor, Lori Zue, who had the courage to tell me when I was going in the wrong direction and expertise to make recommendations.

My deepest appreciation goes to:

Cheerleaders: My cheerleaders kept me going when it seemed like I would never be able to finally finish the book. My husband, Bob New, who never snickered or rolled his eyes when I kept saying, "It's so close to being done." His suggestions and tweaks made what I wrote so much better. My mother, Charleen Bauer, who was an endless source of ideas, articles, and statistics. My sister, Patti Hamilton, who gave me great feedback and coerced her friends to read the book and share their ideas with me.

Champions: These people often believed in me more than I believed in myself. Joe Pici would call me 'out of the blue' and ask me how the book was coming. He was always excited about the book's possibilities. He gave me a bigger vision of what could and will come. Steve Harrison, who's National Publicity Summit allowed me to test-drive the concept of writing a Plan B book when the notion was still just a wispy thought in my head. His ideas and input via the Quantum Leap Program helped shape the concepts of the book and even sparked the title. Countless coaching calls and many valuable gatherings helped me gain my voice and grow my confidence.

Fans: Over twenty reviewers volunteered the time to read and critique the 'final' manuscript. They were blue collar, pink collar and white collar, executives and production workers, retirees and young professionals. They gave me great insights into the final editing of the book.

Divine: There were many times when I was writing it felt like time stood still and I was being guided on what to write. I am certain that I was guided because of a profound sense of knowing that all of my work is going to help countless numbers of people take control of their lives and live their dreams.

As you begin your Plan B 'hero's journey', you too will have many seen and unseen cheerleaders, champions and fans. Come along with me as you start your next adventure!

Plan B Resources and Offers

Go to: www.PlanBCoach.com for a *free assessment* to determine if a Plan B is the right match for you

Also more information on:
Using the **Rich New System**, Kathleen offers coaching and consulting to help you:

- Determine if creating a Plan B is the right decision for you
- Match yourself to the perfect Plan B business
- Learn the language of business
- Avoid the pitfalls of costly and wrong decisions
- Stay focused on the right things in the right order as you launch your new Plan B
- Review your current business operations to identify more profit centers and reduce waste and expenses

Go to www.PlanBCoach.com and sign up for:

- The *Plan B newsletter* giving you new ideas, success stories, and updated information
- Become a *fan* of Plan B's fan page on Facebook
- Attend *Plan B Boot Camps*

A *lot more is coming*…so sign up now so you can be the first

Book Kathleen:

- As a *guest* on your radio or TV show
- As a *key note speaker* at your next event or conference
- For *break out sessions*, half day or full day *training*
- To offer your transitioning employees *more options* when there are few replacement jobs for them

Go to: www.PlanBCoach.com

About the Author

Kathleen Rich-New is the president of Clarity Works Consulting, a human resources firm specializing in a broad spectrum of tactical and strategic human resource practices that include developing human resource strategies to support business goals and objectives.

Kathleen is the go to person that organizations come to for making the right hiring decisions the first time. As a conflict resolution expert she has helped so many businesses redirect their focus from day-to-day management to leadership and strategic plan execution.

In addition to her consulting and coaching business, Kathleen has been an adjunct professor in the Master's programs at Webster University's School of Business & Technology on the Space Coast of Florida for the past 10 years. Kathleen earned a B.S. In Business Administration from the Kansas State University, a M.B.A. in marketing from the University of North Texas (Dr. Phil's alma mater) and a Master's of Management degree in International Human Resources from the University of Dallas.

Earlier in her career, she worked for over 25 years in human resources with companies including Apple Computer, Northern Telecom (Nortel) and Silicon Graphics (SGI.)

Kathleen is co-author of *Looking for the Good Stuff...a guide to enjoying and appreciating life*. She is a contributing columnist for Space Coast Business Magazine and a frequent speaker and writer on human resources and entrepreneurism. Her goal is to share her experience, knowledge and research to help others create their own Plan B.

Index